FANTASY

The Incredible Cabbage Patch Phenomenon

By William Hoffman

FANTASY: The Incredible Cabbage Patch Phenomenon

TEXAS — A YEAR WITH THE BOYS

BEYOND REACH: The Search for the Titanic

DAVID: Report on a Rockefeller

DOCTORS ON THE NEW FRONTIER

PAUL MELLON: Portrait of an Oil Baron

QUEEN JULIANA: The Story of the Richest Woman in
the World

SIDNEY (A Biography of Sidney Poitier)

THE STOCKHOLDER

THE MONEY PLAYER

THE BRIDGE BUM

FANTASY

The Incredible
Cabbage Patch Phenomenon

William Hoffman

Taylor Publishing Company, Dallas, Texas

To Judy Hoffman

Library of Congress Cataloging in Publication Data
Hoffman, William 1937 —
   Fantasy: the incredible Cabbage Patch phenomenon.
   1. Doll industry — United States. 2. Cabbage Patch
Kids dolls. I. Title.
HD9993.D653U64   1984   338.4'76887221'0973   84-8817
ISBN 0-87833-386-X
Printed in the United States of America

First Edition 1 2 3 4 5 6 7 8 9 0

CONTENTS

• 1 •
Cabbage Patch Madness

It was Thanksgiving, a day for turkey and home and family, yet six hours before the 10 A.M. opening of Jefferson Ward department store in North Miami Beach, a crowd began to gather. The black early morning was warm and humid, dark with a threat of rain, but the first arrivals chatted amiably. Although they had never met, they shared a common purpose, and surely this made them brothers and sisters of some sort. There was absolutely no hint of what was soon to erupt.

More people arrived, singly, and in groups of twos and threes. A ragged line slowly formed, snaking back from the department store's doors to the right along the sidewalk and beside freshly scrubbed display windows. There was the expected pushing, jostling, and jockeying for position, but nothing serious, nothing many members of this middle-class, middle-aged crowd hadn't seen before, queuing for tickets at rock concerts: the Beatles, the Stones, Elvis. Here was the 1960s generation grown up, attracted this Thanksgiving by a Jefferson Ward circular:

> Sale priced $21.88. Cabbage Patch Kids
> by Coleco. Sixteen-inch dolls with
> birth certificate, adoption papers, more.
> No two dolls exactly alike!

Still the crowd grew. It packed the sidewalk, its sheer mass spilling people into the roadway and across, washing them into the parking lot packed with cars. The scene was every store owner's dream, a clamoring mass of humanity waving money, super-eager to spend it right then and there.

But the dream abruptly turned to nightmare. The crowd outside started shoving each other, kicking, scratching, even pummeling one another. People began to bang on the doors and windows; the building seemed to shake to its very foundations. Epithets were hurled, fights broke out — what soon would be dubbed around the world as Cabbage Patch Madness — and a visitor from another land might have thought the object being sought was more precious than gold.

Indeed, at this time, the Cabbage Patch Kids did command considerably more value than the $21.88 Jefferson Ward was asking. Some of those in the crowd had been paid to stand there by people known as scalpers, individuals and companies who buy up rare, limited-quantity items and resell them for many times their cost. Super Bowl tickets are such an item, as are ducats for a Michael Jackson concert, though these in all likelihood would never come close to the Cabbage Patch Kids in terms of supply being outstripped by demand. Profits of five hundred percent and more could be turned in a single day by anyone lucky enough to have one of the Kids. Yet it was not financial gain motivating the vast majority outside Jefferson Ward.

The doors of the store opened promptly at 10, and the *Miami Herald* described what happened as a "stampede." Herds of shoppers swept into the store, driven by an invisible prod like cattle to a pen, while others hesitated, not knowing where to go. They were, as store employee Karen Knowles observed, "trampled."

A Miami hurricane might not have been as destructive. Shelves were toppled, displays overturned, merchandise knocked to the floor. So was a 75-year-old man. Jefferson Ward had eighty of the Cabbage Patch Kids, but they were gone in two minutes. There was a lifetime worth of action in those few moments of hysteria.

One of the polyester babies was ripped from its packaging, and two women grabbed it simultaneously. A titanic tug-of-war ensued. One of the women, in a flowered print dress, held the doll by its feet, the other in jeans and halter top, by its head. They strained mightily, huffing and puffing, faces red, muscles bulging in their arms and necks, and when the toy tore apart they were sent reeling backwards. Ms. Jeans-and-Halter Top was cradling the head, and tears tracked down her face. The head she held had belonged to a Kid named Claude Sylvester.

There was something pathetic that pervaded the spectacle. Perhaps the behavior of a heavyset woman in tennis shoes, eyes shaded by a green gambler's visor, best captured the mood of insanity. She stood in the store's aisle, clutching one of the coveted Kids, and whined to no one in particular: "I wanted a girl baby! Not a boy! And I want one with black hair! This baby's hair is brown!"

As the world now knows all too well, Cabbage Patch Kids are never *bought*; they can only be *adopted*. It was, from its inception, a novel marketing concept — some would say the genesis of the doll's singular popularity. The "adoption" is accomplished by the store's "adoption agent" administering the oath to the future "parent" followed by tender of the official "adoption certificate." The oath has read from the beginning:

> After meeting this special Little
> Person Baby and learning his/her needs,
> I want to make the major commitment of becoming
> a good parent to him/her. I solemnly promise
> to be a good parent to my best ability, to
> provide for his/her needs; handle with care;
> love and nourish with most of my affections;
> train him/her up in the way he/she should go;
> and cherish my role as an adoptive parent of
> the only Little Person Baby of his/her kind in
> the world.

With the supply of Cabbage Patch Kids adopted out, those who had been frustrated reacted either with grief or threats. Elizabeth Figueroa, Jefferson Ward toy department employee, said, "Some people were crying because they didn't get one. Some wanted to sue the store because we ran out." Others, even more unruly than when they'd been waiting impatiently outside, kicked counters as they left. Worst of all, a number of shoppers said they wouldn't come to Jefferson Ward again.

* * *

What happened at Jefferson Ward this 1983 Thanksgiving was in no way an isolated occurrence. If anything the tumult was *more* riotous in other areas of South Florida (West Palm Beach, Kendall, Boca Raton, Lauderdale Lakes). For example, fist fights broke out in West Palm Beach as a crowd of more than five hundred, described by bemused witnesses as a "mob," showed up six hours early in the hopes of getting one of only a hundred Kids being offered for adoption. As in North Miami, shoppers in West Palm were trampled, knocked to the ground and run over, in scenes reminiscent of the Iranian revolution.

"They talk about teenagers acting silly at a rock concert," a teenager said. "This beats everything."

It was zany, "wild" he called it, this health-endangering rush of parents to buy a doll (or adopt a baby, if you prefer). It was Cabbage Patch Madness, a sustained, enduring frenzy that gripped much of the American public, more widespread, deep, and lasting than any craze the United States had ever witnessed. A phenomenon. Searching for comparisons, reporters harkened back to the Hula Hoop, the pet rock, the mood ring, the Slinky, but none of these unleashed the breadth of emotions, the *madness*, the bizarre behavior that these homely dolls seemed to elicit. According to promoters of the Kids, the phenomenon is not nearly over. In the words of Casey Stengel, "You ain't seen nothin' yet."

Actually the first Cabbage Patch riot broke out in Philadelphia in late October. Many women's magazines, having just hit the stands, touted the Kids as an excellent Christmas gift idea, and stores were grossly understocked. "Thanks either to [the Philadelphia riot] or to the perspicacity of the PR man who sent a doll to pregnant television host Jane Pauley," wrote *Time* magazine, "the Kids got five-and-a-half minutes of attention on the 'Today' show. Network and local television programs rushed to be next, and Cabbage Patch representatives are still working the talk-show circuit. 'There was some astute PR going on there,' says Rance Crain, editor-in-chief of *Advertising Age*. 'Word of mouth is almost as important in the toy business as it is in the movie business.' And the word was getting around that this was *the* thing to have. By Thanksgiving what had been sellouts became the great Cabbage Patch Panic."

One store manager this Thanksgiving thought it would be irresponsible to open the doors and simply let the crowd thunder inside. "People were pressing on the glass," a store clerk recalled. "People were crying. They were screaming, 'Let me in. Let me in.' "

The manager decided he would pass out numbers to the restless masses, and fearlessly stepped outside. "I started handing out tickets," he recalled, "and there were people all over me. They were grabbing at me, trying to rip the tickets from my hand. They were screaming and tearing at each other. They were going to kill one another just for a doll. I got back inside and called the police."

Having seen that the doors to the store could be opened, the mob grew more frenzied. Sheriff's deputies arrived, but they really could accomplish little. Tear gas a middle-aged, middle-class crowd? Beat them back with clubs? The mentality of the herd prevailed and even the police were swept up in its current. "They were stomping on our feet and kicking us," said Deputy Bud Bonner.

* * *

The Cabbage Patch Kids received literally billions of dollars of free publicity. Not a day went by that they weren't featured on local and national TV news shows, or the big-time talk show circuits. And of course newspapers and magazines were packed with stories. Neighbors talked to neighbors, and strangers could strike up a conversation just by mentioning the dolls. It was revealed that the Little People, cousins of the Cabbage Patch Kids, had been adopted by celebrity parents, including former British Prime Minister Sir Harold Wilson, Linda Blair, Donny and Marie Osmond, Diana Ross, football star Herschell Walker, Tammy Wynette, Engelbert Humperdink, Amy Carter, and Brooke Shields. Nancy Reagan, at the White House, gave two of the dolls to visiting South Korean children. No amount of money in the world could have bought the kind of publicity the Cabbage Patch Kids were receiving free of charge.

Kansas City postman Edward Pennington gave up hope of finding a Kid in the Western Hemisphere and flew to London to adopt one for his five-year-old daughter. The dolls were almost as hot an item in England as in the U.S. — Harrods sold out a supply of one thousand in a little more than an hour, though without any of the chaos or violence often attendant such an event in America — but mailman Pennington succeeded in his pilgrimage overseas. His was not a small victory. Comedian Bob Hope remarked that "Princess Di and Prince Charles couldn't even get one for Christmas." Hope jumped into the fray with a ten-minute skit on his "Christmas Special," featuring Art Carney, Brooke Shields, and Katherine Bach. Hope and Carney played two Mafia types who pull off the Caper of the Century, the kidnapping of the last two Cabbage Patch Kids (Shields and Bach).

The Madness struck Milwaukee, Wisconsin, a no-nonsense, blue-collar city that might not have been expected to fall prey to the mania. Radio announcers Gene Mueller and Bob Reitman of WKTI-FM, as a lark, broadcast that Cabbage Patch Kids would be parachuted out of a B-29 bomber over County Stadium, home of the baseball Brewers, and the "news" sent people scurrying in near-freezing temperatures and 37 mph winds (wind chill seven below zero) to the big ballpark. Many wore catcher's mitts and waved credit cards over their heads. The scene was reminiscent of another hoax, Orson Welles' famous 1930s "War of the Worlds" broadcast, and though WKTI-FM ran disclaimers later in the day (the station was deluged with hundreds of calls), credulous believers remained in the cold and the wind, patting their baseball mitts, eyes lifted skyward, hoping the B-29 pilot would fly overhead.

* * *

The all too frequent sight of individuals willing to risk injury or other physical hardship to obtain one of the scarce babies implanted in the public's mind that here was an object of exceptional worth. Indeed, it was lucky no one did get killed, as the need to possess a Kid, for many, became an overpowering compulsion. At a Caldor Store in Paramus, New Jersey, one woman trying to get to the front of the line for the babies elbowed another woman to near-unconsciousness. In November, in New Jersey, a pregnant woman was buried under an avalanche of shoppers charging a Child World store. A Texas woman clung to her baby though she was being choked by another customer's purse strap. Three hundred shoppers in Concord, New Hampshire, braved freezing cold for five hours to buy dolls totalling one-third the crowd's number, and police had to be called to maintain order. No police were called in Wilkes-Barre, Pennsylvania, and a woman suffered a broken leg.

Many store owners would open their doors just a crack, allow only one customer to enter at a time, and adopt out the dolls individually to people who had been waiting as long as fourteen hours. But even this more sensible plan had its drawbacks: not only was the remainder of the establishment closed for business, but shoppers, spotting the mob from which they had just emerged, were afraid to go back outside again. Carrying a Cabbage Patch Kid through such a throng could be as dangerous as strolling through a darkened Central Park sporting expensive jewelry.

"I think they're dangerous," said Larry Hotchkiss, a Best Products Company manager who was threatened by an enraged mob at the rear of his Dallas, Texas, store. Snarling customers demanded that Hotchkiss unload a crate of just-arrived dolls and adopt them out on the spot.

"It's like watching a football game," decided Chip Tate, a personnel manager at Alexander's in Greenville, South Carolina. He had stood amazed as fifty people gave a credible imitation of two football teams scrambling for a loose ball with six Cabbage Patch Kids having initiated the scrimmage. Tate watched open-mouthed as one shopper managed to gather three into her arms — a feat that would have given any Pro scout pause — only to then stand oblivious to the battle raging around her, deliberating about which one she wanted.

Football actually was part of a scenario in Des Moines, Iowa. An eighty-year-old grandmother wanted to give one of the Kids to her young great-granddaughter, but she'd seen and read about the danger facing shoppers foolhardy enough to brave the inflamed crowds. She asked her grandson, a football player at the University of Iowa, if he could help, and he devised a clever tactic. When the store opened, with two of his football buddies running interference (dropping out at prearranged stations), the grandson beat the stampede to the Cabbage Patch display. He then lobbed a picture-perfect spiral over the heads of the mob to his first friend, who in turn was on target to the second friend waiting at the checkout counter. On Christmas morning, the four-year-old great-granddaughter declared that the Cabbage Patch Kid "was what she'd always wanted."

It was not only the consumer who faced bodily harm in a Cabbage Patch run. A Pennsylvania Zayre department store manager, William Shigo, armed himself with a baseball bat, saying, "This is my life that's in danger!" The baseball bat was a sensible precaution in view of the 1,000 people, some of whom had been waiting for eight hours, that were massed menacingly outside Zayre's. Miraculously, casualties numbered only five this day, the most serious being a broken leg.

One thousand people must have seemed child's play to Scott Belcher, manager of Hill's Department Store in Charleston, West Virgina, where *five thousand* shoppers stormed his establishment for Cabbage Patch Kids whose availability numbered one hundred and twenty. "They knocked over tables," shuddered Belcher, "fighting with each other — there were people in midair. It got ugly."

Unwilling to go to such lengths, some people shopped for the Kids by telephone. "I get sixty or seventy calls a day for them," said Wayne Dugger, manager of Toy Fair Big Town in Mesquite, Texas. Dugger said his store had mercifully been spared destruction. "But if I had one hundred dolls and put them all out there on the floor, I imagine you'd see a riot."

Wayne Dugger didn't know what demand is. Store manager Ron Laughon of Best Products in Dallas said his store received 400 to 600 calls a day. "If I could get five thousand," Laughon said, referring to the Cabbage Patch Kids, "I still couldn't keep them in stock. I spend my whole day on the phone saying, 'I'm sorry, I'm sold out, I'm sorry, I'm sold out.' Even though I'd love to get some more of the dolls, at least without them I'm not having any fights in the store."

Although possession of Cabbage Patch Kids guaranteed a big crowd at your store, not every retail outlet wanted a supply. Neiman-Marcus of Houston, for example, has sold such exotic items as a $3,500 custom-designed mousetrap which traps mice alive in a miniature ranch, a 106-carat opal said to be designed by Pliny the Elder (cost $150,000), and something for the person who has everything, a submarine (price tag $1 million). Neiman-Marcus professed even to be happy about having neglected to order the Christmas season's hottest product. "Who needs hysteria at this time of the year?" asked Edward Bode, Neiman-Marcus manager.

Other stores decided to *give* the Kids away rather than risk having their stores ransacked. "We saw all the bedlam at other stores," said Roy E. Boutillier, director of marketing at Gimbels Midwest, who donated his supply to Milwaukee Children's Hospital.

* * *

The Cabbage Patch Kids was that rare product that needed no advertising. Riots in stores guaranteed the babies would be kept in the news, and, in any case, they were as popular a subject of conversation as the weather. Coleco made heroic efforts, airlifting the Kids from Hong Kong via 747s, to at least stay within distant sight of demand, but it was an impossible task. Inexplicably, Coleco continued to advertise the Kids, bringing upon itself the wrath of New York's Nassau County consumer affairs department. This government agency filed a false-advertising charge, and contended Coleco was "harrassing" children by running ads for dolls which were not available. Coleco quickly cooperated and discontinued further advertising.

One reason the Kids were in short supply was that they often never reached the store shelves. They would be adopted by store employees as soon as they arrived, or put aside for favored customers. At the New York City Macy's, the largest department store in the U.S., 150 arrivals were grabbed up before the doors opened. "The trick with a hot property like this," wrote *Fortune* magazine, December 26, 1983, "is to practice birth control, keeping supply just short of demand in hopes that the dolls will over time become another classic like Barbie. As Coleco admits, the birth control this year was inadvertently severe. It plans to boost production from 2.5 million this year to perhaps twice that in 1984, when the partners in the Patch hope to see $1 billion in retail sales."

Fortune magazine may have understated. There is informed talk that as many as *twelve million* of the Kids may be born in 1984. Where the magazine might have hit the mark was in the comparison to the early Barbies, now greatly increased in value. Collectors of the Little People (upon whom the Cabbage Patch Kids are modeled), the hand-stitched, soft-sculpture "babies" which first appeared in 1977, have seen their original investment balloon as much as four thousand percent.

So, it was not just Coleco fattening up on Cabbage Patch Madness. A single edition of the *Washington Post* carried forty-eight classified ads for the dolls, with asking prices ranging from as low as $30 for a Cabbage Patch Kid to $3,000 for a Little Person. The latter was placed by Jalynn Prince of Bethesda, Maryland, and she didn't sound too eager to put the baby up for readoption. "I have already received two offers that sound pretty concrete," Ms. Prince said. "Even if I get the price I want, I would have to make sure the doll was going to good people."

Another *Washington Post* ad offered a brother and sister set for the highest offer over $2,000. They had to be bought as a set because the sellers "will not separate the family." Another brother and sister combo were offered for $2,500, and came with a free 1948 pickup truck "to take them home in."

A number of peripheral institutions, as well as individuals, found ways to cash in on the craze. The Gwinnett County Bank outside Atlanta persuaded more than five hundred big persons to deposit some $2 million in its vaults by offering half-priced Little People as premiums. A Kansas radio station experienced skyrocketing ratings when it chartered an airplane to fly eighteen Cabbage Patch Kids, each with its own seat, from Dallas as part of a promotional giveaway. In another example of commercial use of the phenomenon, Emery Air Freight ran full-page newspaper ads, headlined "To Keep Up With These Kids You've Gotta Be Fast," which read: "The Cabbage Patch Kids craze has the nation going ga-ga. These homely but huggable little soft sculptures are setting all-time records for doll sales in an introductory year. This is one instance, in fact, in which the demand has actually exceeded the supply.

"Faced with this unusual dilemma, the manufacturer, Coleco Industries, is doing everything possible to avoid disappointing a single child. That's why we at Emery are proud to have been entrusted with the safe and speedy delivery of these special kids."

Other commercial ads appeared spontaneously in newspapers all over the country. A full-page ad in the *Philadelphia Inquirer*, paid for by Pacifico Ford, said that for one day only the dealership would throw in a Cabbage Patch Kid for anyone who buys a new car.

Also the following ad appeared in the *Dallas Morning News:*

> Help, Help! I'm being held
> captive along with all my Cabbage
> Patch friends at Jim Allee Oldsmobile.
> Mrs. Allee has promised only to
> let us go to the first 48 warm
> and loving families who buy any
> new or used car before December 23, 1983.

Mark Demmer, sales manager, says that people, on occasion, are still asking about the Kids.

A Cabbage Patch Kid auctioned for charity in San Diego, California, brought $2,200. Four Cabbage Patch Kids were auctioned in Irving, Texas, for $5,000 to help pay for the liver transplant of three-year-old Jonathon Lehman. All of these were Cabbage Patch Kids, not the more expensive Little People, which regularly are readopted to collectors for thousands of dollars.

But nothing, absolutely nothing, topped the price asked for a Cabbage Patch Kid by Cartier Jewelers in Beverly Hills, California. The baby's name was Aretha Flori, she came with a sapphire necklace, diamond bracelet, and diamond earrings on her shoes. The adoption fee: $35,000.

* * *

The zeal exhibited by millions of people to adopt the babies carries over, for many of them, to taking care of them. Many of the "parents" treat the dolls as if they are real children. A Rome, Georgia, housewife, Patricia Alexander, charged $10 a week to babysit *one* of them, and her nursery averaged almost a dozen boarders at any given time. "In the adoption papers," Ms. Alexander pointed out, "it says you agree not to leave the babies alone."

Damaged ("injured" or "sick," Cabbage Patch parents would call them) dolls are often brought hundreds and even thousands of miles to Babyland General Hospital in Cleveland for treatment, which includes surgery. The staff at Babyland, dressed as doctors and nurses (protocol says you should address each as "Doctor" or "Nurse"), are accustomed to handling emergencies. A Cincinnati, Ohio, couple suffered when their Little Person was run over by a truck and *drove all the way to Georgia* to see if the "child" could be saved. She couldn't be.

The Brindel family enjoys dining out; and Don Brindel, a marketing manager for Allis-Chalmers Corporation, takes his daughter's doll, Eudora, along with them, seating her in a high chair at the restaurant table. Eudora is "part of the family," Don Brindel explains.

Mickey Benamy of Atlanta, Georgia, is another who talks to his doll. The baby's name is Derek, and most nights Benamy straps him into the front seat of his silver Cadillac Eldorado and "bounces ideas off him" as the two drive along together. Derek is the perfect listener.

Mickey Benamy's Derek has his own room, but this would be impossible at Jessye Schleiffarth's home in Baton Rouge. She has ninety-two of the dolls, and says, "I feel like I'm living in Munchkinland." Cheryl McCain, a mother of two in Douglasville, Georgia, said she adopted her "baby" because "this was easier labor" than having a real child.

Helen Biever of Cumming, Georgia, has made provisions in her will for the disposition of the dolls. Roy Capobianco of Whitestone, New York, who has twenty dolls, says, "They are the only possession of ours that I would never sell. They are a part of my family." Janet Darmofal, Kissimmee, Florida, owner of thirteen babies, wanted to get into the business of adopting them out. "The only problem," she says, "is that I'd cry as each one left me. I love them all so very much. I can't picture any day without them."

* * *

What kind of gifts are the Cabbage Patch Kids? ALTER-NATIVES, a Georgia-based non-profit group, determined to take the commercialization out of Christmas, takes nominations each year for the most crass, the most tasteless presents offered to the public each Christmas season. They elected the Kids as the worst present one could put under the tree, beating out a Santa Claus tobacco tin and, believe it or not, edible underwear. "The Cabbage Patch Kids," said ALTERNATIVES, "were nominated by many, many people. The dolls clearly brought out the worst in consumers, who trampled one another in a frenzy of Christmas spirit to purchase the dolls."

People magazine called the Cabbage Patch Madness "dog-eat-dog anarchy." The *Wall Street Journal* said it was "mass hysteria." Dr. Ralph Wittenberg, chairman of the public-information committee of the Washington, D.C., Psychiatric Society, was concerned about "phenomena when people get the impression that there is something very precious and special about something or someone. You somehow submerge your independent observation and judgment to some more authoritative person or more powerful event." Dr. Wittenberg recognized in the fanatic crowds the underpinnings of other similarly strong and negative social movements such as, for example, Nazism.

Yet the consumer affairs committee of Americans for Democratic Action (ADA), a more liberal organization, praised the Kids as one of the most creative toys of the 1983 holiday season. The babies received high marks not only for being exceptionally safe to play with, but for conveying the message that "you don't have to be beautiful to be loved." Columnist and psychologist Dr. Joyce Brothers gave the Cabbage Patch Kids an unreserved endorsement. But regardless of what self-styled experts said, citizens themselves were speaking loud and clear, and they couldn't be ignored.

* * *

Riots. Attempts at bribery. Serious personal injuries. Extensive property damage. Bizarre individual and group behavior. All of this and more played a part in the Incredible Cabbage Patch Phenomenon but none of it seems out of the ordinary in comparison to the sudden, stunning success experienced by the 28-year-old father of these millions of babies, the man who unwittingly created an international rage.

Xavier and the Little People

The *Wall Street Journal,* during the 1983 Christmas Madness, worried where it was all taking us:

We have no doubt whatsoever what the outcome would be if the proprietors of, say, the Washington Post/ABC Poll were to ask 1,200 American families with children under the age of reason the following single question — What currently is of greatest concern to you: a) the threat of extinction in a nuclear war; or b) the acquisition of a Cabbage Patch Kid before Dec. 25?

Unquestionably, the response would be: a) 1%; b) 99%

We do not cite the inevitable results of such a poll merely to score cheap points against our opponents in the nuclear-deterrence debate. We do so in the belief that as citizens of a great nation, it behooves each of us to come to terms with the Cabbage Patch Kids.

We are the people who the president calls the world's "last best hope." We are the people who put a man on the moon. And we are the people who are now breaking down the doors of every toy store in America, threatening the proprietors with death and chop-blocking each other to buy our children a Cabbage Patch Kid — a 16-inch, $20 doll said to come from Babyland General Hospital with adoption papers and its own disposable diaper. It appears that every child in America wants one for Christmas.

Coleco Industries did not make enough of them. The law of supply and demand has broken down, and the aisles of Toys "R" Us are beginning to look like the streets of Beirut.

Where it was taking us might have been difficult to say, but it is easy to locate where it began. . . .

Xavier Roberts was born in 1955 on Halloween, day of fantasy and make-believe, at Habersham County Hospital, the sixth and last child of Harold and Eula Roberts of Cleveland, Georgia. Xavier was lucky to have had a hospital birth. Three of his five brothers and sisters had been delivered at home, and the same had been planned for him. But Xavier arrived prematurely, and the parents, fearing complications, chose the safest, albeit more expensive, route. The stay in the hospital was a rare taste of luxury for Eula.

At the suggestion of Eula's brother, John, the healthy seven-pound baby was named Xavier, which sounded "real different" to the mother, and was for a family which is not Roman Catholic. No one in the family knew how to spell "Xavier," so the name on the birth certificate read "Ernest Exavery Roberts." It was years before the error was corrected. (Reading was not a high priority in the Roberts home, so it was not surprising the family could not spell "Xavier." Years later Xavier would confess that it was a long time before he could correctly spell the name of his own corporation, Original Appalachian Artworks.)

The Roberts family was poor. Poor as in North Georgia mountain poor, where the towns are small, the rural dwellings far apart, and industrial work and wages something other areas of the state or nation get. Harold Roberts, the father, known to everyone in Cleveland as "Happy," had, like his wife, a less-than-grade-school education, and eked out a living for his family doing carpentry jobs. Eula, who met Happy when she was fifteen and he twenty-one, had her hands full at home. Her family was growing by leaps and bounds, and there never seemed to be enough money. There wasn't.

Eula, who lost one child, gave birth to Barbara, Vivian,

Harold, Jerry, John, and finally Xavier. Her strength was her religion, and each Sunday the Roberts clan filled a pew at the nearby Baptist church, where the religion was the good old-fashioned kind. As the family struggled to keep body and soul together, there was nothing, nothing whatsoever, to indicate that one of its number would grow up to be an enormous international financial success.

For her part, Eula Roberts excelled at quilting. Anyone seeing her work would be stunned by its beauty. Although Eula won numerous awards for her quilts, there really wasn't a way to make a living from her craft. Quilting, at its best, is difficult, painstaking labor, and the uninitiated might wonder why anyone in modern America would undertake it, when buying a blanket from a store is so much cheaper.

The quilt itself is basically a simple project. It consists of a bottom lining, usually a stuffing of cotton or home-grown wool, a top lining and the top itself. "But there," writes Eliot Wigginton in *The Foxfire Book*, "the simplicity stops. The top was made of a number of separate squares joined either side to side, or separated from each other by cloth borders. Thus a quilt that measured sixty by eighty inches might take forty-eight 10-inch squares, sixteen 13-inch ones, or any of a number of combinations. Each square was usually identical in pattern but distinctive in color. All the squares for one quilt might be made by the same person, or they might be made by a number of different individuals who later got together to produce the final work. Sizes varied according to the beds the quilts were to fit, or the requirements of the individuals for whom they were being made."

"You check on it," said North Georgian, Bess McBrayer, herself an expert at quilting, "and you'll find that Xavier inherited his artistic ability from his Momma."

Xavier readily admits it. And he also admits that his tenacity likely came from Eula. The almost infinite patience required to stitch intricate patterns into a blanket, the sheer quality of being able to stay with something which is difficult for a long time, is a virtue not to be underestimated. Your eyes begin to sting, and your back is on fire; the bones in your fingers and hands hurt beyond belief. Understandably, top-drawer quilts have been known to take years to produce.

The assertion that "If you can't be creative here, you won't be creative anywhere" could have been made about Cleveland, Georgia, and its environs. Not far from Cleveland is Brasstown Bald, highest point in Georgia, 4,784 feet above sea level, and on a clear day you can see four states, plus the misted magnificence of the Blue Ridge Mountains. The area is idyllic, straight out of a child's fantasyland, a place of almost surpassing beauty. Although renowned for its lovely Autumn when the mountain frost turns leaves to brilliant yellows and reds, each season has its own special beauty. The grass is the bright green of Ireland's, the air brisk and bracing, marvelous to fill the lungs with, and the sheer natural beauty can take one's breath away.

Georgia's poet laureate, Sidney Lanier (1842-1881), immortalized the area with his "Song of the Chattahoochee," and so did the legend of Princess Nacoochee and Prince Sautee. These two Indians, from the warring Cherokee and Chickasaw tribes, were refused permission to marry by their fathers, and ran off together. Cornered on the top of Mount Yonah, Sautee was thrown off a cliff to his death by members of the Cherokee tribe. Showing the ultimate love, Princess Nacoochee broke free from her captors and leaped from the cliff to join Sautee. The two chiefs, deeply affected by the devotion of the two young people for each other, declared a halt to the fighting between the tribes. Sautee and Nacoochee were buried in an earthen shrine still visible near what is now the town of Helen. The land is full of myth and magic, which has informed the culture and shaped the people's imagination.

White County was the site of America's first gold discovery, in 1829, and when the boom petered out thirty years later most of the Indians had been rounded up and herded away. Their confinement to reservations in the West, recurring again and again, became infamous as "The Trail of Tears" and "The Trail of Broken Treaties." Anyone doubting the influence of early Indians (there is Cherokee blood in Xavier) on the arts and crafts of North Georgia should visit Brasstown Bald, where the evidence of Native American cultural contributions is manifest at every turn.

The county seat of White County, Helen, is just ten miles from Cleveland, and this picturesque little town also left its mark on the young Xavier, though today it bears little resemblance to what he remembers as a boy. Now a visitor to Helen, Georgia, might think he had been dropped suddenly into an Alpine village in Bavaria. The town has been completely transformed, packed with charming gingerbread houses and cobblestoned streets, window boxes filled with flowers. There are numerous Old World candy, bakery, and cheese shops. Along with an Oktoberfest, there is now a thriving summer theater, square dancing, folk singing, and a bountiful offering of locally made mountain wares.

The Roberts children had the pleasant fortune of being surrounded by art. They lived right in the center of this active, vibrant, dynamic community of mountain artisans and artists unspoiled by commercial success and its Coca-Cola culture demands. So unlike the more urbane environment of a museum or a gallery, it was as if in these beautiful north Georgia foothills of the Appalachian Mountains a community of greatly talented people had suddenly sprung forth (though, of course, their forebears had been there for centuries, their roots having taken in the area's prehistory, with the Cherokee and Chickasaw). When Lady Bird Johnson visited White (where Cleveland is located) and surrounding counties during her husband's tenure as president she came away awed by the talent of these simple mountain folk. But it had been there all the time, the dazzling arts and crafts, the magnificent woodworking, weaving, antiquing, painting, pottery, and quilting. It was not the people's fault they had not been discovered. They were too busy *doing*.

When Happy Roberts courted Eula, he had to walk several miles round trip to and from her home, and after the marriage walking continued to be the normal mode of transportation. Happy-go-lucky applied to Xavier's father, and though he would never have much luck, very little if anything depressed him.

Eula was the serious one. To her Happy sometimes seemed more like another child than a parent. He loved to romp in the woods with the kids — more a friend than a father — play games with them, join them in youthful pranks. Though Eula was sometimes exasperated by his behavior, they had a good marriage, and on his serious side, he was able to teach rudimentary carpentry skills to his older boys.

The Roberts family finally purchased a car (Happy's work was now steady enough that they could even consider buying a modest home), but he was so accustomed to walking that he once forgot he had driven it to work and came all the way home on foot. It was unfortunate the memory lapse did not reoccur on August 19, 1960.

It was raining, a hard, dark, dangerous rain, and Happy, driving alone from work, less than a mile from home, hit a wet spot and skidded onto the grassy shoulder. The car swerved back onto the road, flipping over three times, and smashed into a tree. Happy was dead before the ambulance ever got there.

Eula had a minimal education, six children, no money. She landed a minimum-wage job at Ames Textiles and dug in for permanent hard times.

Xavier, five years old when Happy died, remembers very little about his father. His sisters cared for him while his mother worked. There was religion, and as much love as an exhausted mother could provide, and little else.

The early years in school were rough; Xavier was small for his age, and classmates razzed him unmercifully about his name. For a time he thought of changing it, but never did. He was also harassed for being poor, as if that were some crime, for the clothes he wore, for anything that young, unthinking children can find that is hurtful. But being poor bothered him the most. And it bothered Eula.

I told my mother I was going to be the richest person in the world at whatever I did," Xavier says.

"Did she believe you?"

"She said she did."

At age ten Xavier wanted to join the Boy Scouts, but buying a uniform was simply out of the question. It was a struggle just to eat. A scoutmaster eventually made the purchase for Xavier, but somehow the news leaked to other members of the troop, and he quit the Boy Scouts, never to return.

Xavier enjoyed walking alone in the woods and hills, fishing in the Chattahoochee River, sitting at his mother's side as she taught him fashion design and quilt-making. Much of the time he resembled a dreamy loner, by himself and lost in his own thoughts. What he did acquire was a deep hatred of poverty, and more important, an almost fanatical willingness to work hard to escape it. In this Eula offered no discouragement.

"I wasn't too smart in school," Xavier probably understates. "My only 'A's' were in art. I used to make things — pots and clay figures, kind of wild things — and sell them to the other students.

Early on Xavier decided he wanted to be an artist, but unlike many youngsters, who dream of being firemen or baseball players or doctors, his goal never changed. He had talent and a drive to work long hours, and a powerful urge to accumulate money. Surely life could be more than a dreary struggle with never two nickels to rub together?

Xavier had a worm's-eye view of money. "I always thought," he told this author, driving through the north Georgia countryside, "that 'riches' was the guy in Cleveland with the brick house." When he became enormously wealthy — thirty-bedroom house, a fleet of Mercedes-Benzes, lucrative real estate holdings, a hundred shootoffs from his spectacularly flourishing doll empire — he professed never to be surprised. "I knew I'd be rich," he said. "I dreamed about it and aimed for it. I just never knew what rich was."

Eula, of course, was the quiet heroine behind all of this. She was considered poor by any standard, but she kept the family going and together. To support her large brood she worked late into the night quilting, dead tired from her factory job, to earn the difference that meant eating or not.

"As he got a little older," Eula says, "I would watch Xavier work so hard, trying to make something out of what little he had. He'd go out in the fields and collect wild flowers that he'd fix up nice with a piece of driftwood and sell. I would help him make quilts that he'd take up to Tallulah Falls Craft Shop and sell."

It was at this juncture he learned he was *good* at selling. Book learning — he seldom read books — he might be weak at, but he had his art, from Eula and from the very air he breathed. And he could *sell*.

Xavier marched to a different drummer. He enjoyed cooking, especially pecan pies (the pecans are unmatched in Georgia), and, says Eula, "His older brothers didn't always think too much of what he was doing, but I did." His older brothers did make fun of his efforts in the kitchen, just as classmates joked about his name and his family's lack of money, but the gibes never hurt enough to make him stop.

White County High School, which Xavier entered in 1969, had only a one-year art course, but by helping his art instructor, Connie Schapanski, he was able to gain access to paints and supplies that otherwise he could never have afforded. Like many of the self-made rich, the original John D. Rockefeller, for example, Eula's youngest was absolutely singleminded, close-to-the-vest with money, and willing to labor unlimited hours to attain his objectives.

"Xavier never gave up,"Eula remembers. "In high school, he got a job at the Tastee Freeze and worked until eleven at night, helping out with family expenses."

Xavier, graduating in 1973, was voted "Most Talented" member of his senior class, but what he really wanted was to go to college and have the opportunity to continue his art studies. It was impossible. He didn't have the money and neither did his family. The only answer was to work and save, the work being no problem at all for the young man willing to go to any lengths to be rich and successful. Being poor, being reminded he was poor, had left a lasting mark.

He worked first at Ames Textiles, then as a carpenter with his older brothers, saving every cent he could from the low-paying jobs, and in his spare time he made a variety of mountain art forms. Sixteen months after he left high school, now age eighteen, in the Autumn of 1974, he had enough money to enroll at Truett-McConnell College in Cleveland to major in art.

Xavier's cash ran out during his second quarter, and it looked like it was back to carpentry for another year until enough money could be saved. But at the last minute a Basic Educational Opportunity Grant (BEOG) he had applied for came through, permitting him to continue into the Spring quarter, 1975. There would be other dramatic last-instant reprieves for Xavier, particularly when the business he was to found was first gaining its feet. "If you think you can, you can," Xavier likes to say. But he had his share of luck, also. And timing.

In the Summer of 1975, as a requirement of the BEOG program, Xavier started an internship as a crafts counsellor at Unicoi State Park, which is near Brasstown Bald. Unicoi State Park is a beautiful place, situated on a forested slope above a 52-acre lake. One can listen to soulful folk-singing, evocative of the no-frills life still very much a part of the mountains, or watch pottery and quilting demonstrations, go canoeing or on nature walks. There are cottages, tent and trailer camping, facilities for picnics and swimming, and especially marvelous planned programs of nature and environmental studies, with particular emphasis on arts and crafts.

Xavier worked in the craft shop. He sold local artwork, and soon decided he would display and try to sell his own creations — his quilting and pottery — in the shop. His pay at the gift shop was $60 a week, but people occasionally purchasing his work helped supplement the income.

It was still a daily struggle to stay in school, but Xavier was back at Truett-McConnell in the Autumn of 1975, trying to expose himself to as many varieties of art as possible. He concentrated on pottery, but also learned macramé, weaving, and hand-woven wall hangings.

January, 1976, was the beginning of the first real breakthrough. Not yet twenty-one years old, Xavier read in an old dog-eared library book about a German folk art, dating to the early nineteenth century, called "needle molding." Today it is known as "soft sculpture," but whatever the preferred name, Xavier realized it was similar to what his mother had been doing creating those beautiful quilts. "I sure understood about soft sculpture," he said, remembering what he had seen Eula so often accomplish. "I started making soft-sculpture plants and wall hangings, then pigs and clowns, experimenting. I'd had a teddy bear as a little boy. They're cuddly. People like nice soft friendly things to hold." Soon the young artist wanted to try the human form, using his nieces and nephews as models.

Xavier went to Eula for help. "My mother," he said, "showed me how to sew, to mold the fabric. It was like working with clay. I made them [the human forms] by hand using a four-way stretch fabric, stuffed them with soft fibers, stitched the mouths, painted the eyes, every one different. I still have one of the first. Otis Lee has been with me through thick and thin.

"I called them Little People. We used to say we found them in a cabbage patch. You know that's what mothers tell their children when they ask, 'Where did I come from?' "

In October, 1976, Xavier was promoted to manager of the Unicoi State Park gift shop, and his college days were almost over. Persistently an idea kept rearing its head that had nothing to do with continuing and finishing school: he was now devoting most of his time to soft sculpture, particularly the human form; more particularly, babies.

"The babies fascinated me," he remembers. "I couldn't believe the expressions I got with stitching. A tuck here, a pucker there, and the whole face took on life. Cloth is like clay. You can just touch it and see something happen."

As he'd done earlier with his pottery and quilting, Xavier took his soft sculture dolls to the Unicoi gift shop and arranged them in a lifelike display. He says he really didn't intend to sell them, that he just wanted to see the reaction they would elicit. It came quickly and as a surprise.

"How much are these dolls?" a visitor to the craft shop wanted to know.

Well, they're not for sale." Into his mind popped visions of being poor. "But you can adopt them," he added quickly. "For thirty dollars."

Thirty dollars was a lot of money to Xavier. He wondered what the woman would say.

"I'll take this one. By the way, . . ." She asked if he could sculpt a doll from a photograph.

Indeed he could. He asked for sixty dollars more and the woman willingly agreed to pay.

Out of this initial transaction was born the idea of adopting the dolls out, not merely selling them; it would turn out to be a stroke of marketing genius. That it didn't start out cynically in the mind of some Madison Avenue type probably explains the reason for its freshness. In reality, Xavier was quite taken with his own early work, and flirted with the thought of keeping it. "I didn't want them to be toys. Children are so spoiled today. I was afraid they'd tear them up in two days. So I thought up the idea of the adoption certificate and the pledge they'd take care of the kids."

Early in 1977, having just turned twenty-one, Xavier found himself to be a one-man band with more requests than he could fill, even working the eighteen-hour days he was more than willing to put in. "At first," he says, "I really liked delivering the babies. I was adopting the bald ones for fifty dollars, and those with hair for sixty dollars. But soon there were more orders than I could handle. I asked my mother and sisters to come in and start helping me out, but orders continued to exceed our capacity to fill them."

Xavier had started on a roller-coaster ride which would propel him to spectactular heights; but along the way there also would be dizzying turns and dangerous, sudden drops. It helped that he was caught up in his own adoption fantasy.

The longer a person engages in make-believe, the more that "world" is likely to become real to him. It is common in children, who for much of a day may become Superman or Spiderman or Tarzan, but it happens to adults, too. Married couples frequently asssume different personas, not only in love relationships but in the run-of-the-mill routine of day-to-day living. Living a fantasy became the norm for Xavier. He could no more call his dolls "dolls" than Fonzie on "Happy Days" could bring himself to say "I'm afraid." Every waking hour Xavier thought of how he could create a whole world for his babies, a wonderland more elaborate than any fantasy a fiction writer could construct, and calling a doll a baby became as easy to him as saying hello. He could talk endlessly to "prospective parents" about the desires and dislikes of his Kids — what they like to eat, the games they play, their thoughts about school — a tireless exposition with no other boundaries than the imagination. Most people, first hearing Xavier, would think it was silliness, or that the young artist was "a bit tetched." Most people, listening long enough, joined in the fantasy.

Now, only twenty-one-years-old, Xavier Roberts, using as a model his own birth certificate, painstakingly drew up an individualized version for the Little People and took it along with him to the gift shop at Unicoi State Park. It immediately drew attention and comment. In March, 1977, he ordered the printing of one thousand blue-bordered birth certificates (for a thousand dolls which didn't exist), plus manila-colored name tags to attach to the front of them. It was by far the largest investment Xavier had ever made, completely exhausting his small savings, and he remembers holding his breath hoping there would be a payoff.

Xavier hand-printed the name tags, listed the location of the births as Babyland General Hospital (a place that didn't exist), and the town of the births as Helen, Georgia. Each doll as it was made had "footprints" stamped on its bottom, the footprints actually being impressions of Xavier's fist and fingertips, and each was autographed and numbered. Anyone who bought one of these original thousand dolls was blessed with great acumen, foresight, or luck. They sold for thirty dollars and may be worth three thousand dollars today.

Names for the original dolls were taken from a 1937 baby book. (Names would become a problem later on — millions have been manufactured, and the promise is given that no two have the same name — but no difficulty existed at the beginning.) These original dolls were different from those being made today. "We were experimenting and just having fun with it," says Xavier. "There was no set pattern at the time."

Affording clothes for the dolls seemed almost an insurmountable obstacle. Xavier haunted flea markets and yard sales from which he could clothe his babies, scavenged about for hand-me-downs and other used attire no one else wanted. And there was the problem of distribution. Surely he would not be able to distribute and sell a thousand relatively expensive dolls at the Unicoi State Park craft shop, where his position as employee could not be confused with that of an owner who could stock as much of whatever he wanted. The problem was further complicated in that Xavier was not yet willing to take the ultimate gamble of striking out on his own with his dolls. Truett-McConnell College was a memory of the past, but he clung to the security of his craft shop job.

A college friend, Debbie Morehead, had been listed as the "mother" of the first thousand babies. Debbie was herself an artist of talent and promise, and in May, 1977, she helped Xavier pack his battered Volkswagen with dolls and her watercolors and the two headed for a nearby art show where they had rented a booth.

Xavier stole the show. It was partly the atmosphere he created, partly his own gregarious nature, partly that the dolls were indeed hand-made original works of art. He had a flair for display, carefully positioning his babies in playpens, high chairs, cribs, wagons, on tiny tricycles, asleep or standing up, arms extended as if asking to be held. A child's nursery really looked like a child's nursery, a sandbox like a sandbox. It was as if shoppers had happened upon a real-life world, though of course it was fantasy. And Xavier would talk to everybody, spinning yarns about the babies, their humble beginnings in the cabbage patch, their aspirations for a good, loving home. "When is his birthday?" someone asked at this first art show. "Today," Xavier ad-libbed. "And a year from today we'll send him a birthday card." Just so, on the spur of the moment, was another marketing coup conceived. People thought they were getting something free, and the idea of their babies having their birthdays remembered seemed appealing and delighted prospective parents. Finally, each doll was different, you could see it just by looking; there was none of the cookie-cutter sameness of, say, Barbie. Nor were the dolls bland, i.e., cute and winsome yet vacuous. Some thought they were ugly. Others believed their charms grew on you. Whatever, as one person said, "They're not perfect. In that respect they're like human beings."

Xavier gave his dolls the collective name "Little People."

The first art show Debbie Morehead and Xavier attended reinforced his impression that he wasn't alone in believing his soft-sculpture babies were special. He'd seen the reactions at the Unicoi craft shop, and now they'd been repeated. Hungry for success — for money more than success — he increased efforts that already bordered on the prodigious.

Xavier managed the craft shop during the week, and each weekend saw him on the road, Debbie Moreland and her paintings at his side, traveling to art shows, shoppng centers, country fairs, driving the beat-up Volkswagen to every conceivable place where he might show off his babies. Xavier was tireless. The distance he could separate himself from his childhood poverty, from the taunts of playmates, was measured by money.

Debbie and Xavier would start each weekend before dawn (or Friday after work sometimes) and they didn't stop. Xavier seemed always on a high, talking up his babies, careful ever to be certain they were properly displayed; he was like an ambitious Southern politician wanting to shake every hand in the county, get his name and particularly his babies known. Stopping for breath — ever — wasn't part of the campaign.

"Everybody thought I was crazy," Xavier says. "But I sold them at flea markets and craft fairs. First for thirty dollars each. That's a lot of money. And then so many people wanted them — all over the Southeast, they'd follow me around — I had to go up to fifty dollars, sixty dollars, one hundred and twenty-five dollars. First I hired three school friends, girls, to help Mother and me make them."

In spite of substantial price increases, no one, not a single person, who adopted an early baby has had the slightest cause for complaint. Most products run out, wear out, or break down. They *decrease* in value (in the case of an automobile, the moment you drive out of the showroom). What Xavier produced was more like a money-printing machine, except better: you didn't have to do anything but play with it or watch it sit there and *increase* in value.

He and Debbie Moreland were hitting every craft show they could find within the driving distance of the ancient Volkswagen. They were barely making ends meet. What money the dolls brought in had immediately to go back out for materials and supplies. Occasionally the two slept in the tiny car to keep expenses down. The days which stretched into nights were long and exhausting, brutal under a hot Georgia sun. They were especially so for Debbie, who seemed not to possess her friend's boundless reserves of energy and enthusiasm.

Xavier considered it a learning process. He was learning that his babies were popular *everywhere*, not just in the White County mountain country. Everywhere his Volkswagen could get him, that is.

There are numerous skilled artisans in Cleveland and its environs, producing folk art and crafts that dazzle the eye and excite the mind. But the work never seems to get much further than North Georgia. One of Xavier's strokes of genius was the realization that if the world wouldn't come to him, he'd go out and introduce himself.

Xavier wanted another test. The people he met told him

they loved his creations, often backed their words up with "adoption fees," but what did they really know? And although he thought the babies were art, what did he know? Truett-McConnell College was not the Sorbonne,and just how much had Cleveland, Georgia, art instructors, and his mother, taught him?

In October, 1977, the loyal Debbie Morehead at his side, Xavier decided to make the long drive to Kissimmee, Florida, near Disney World, to enter his work into competition at the Osceola Craft Show. Artists from all over the south would compete for prizes and coveted recognition. A victory would be a big feather in his cap, though Xavier had no idea what he could expect from the professional judges.

One of his quilts won a $200 award. But far more important, a bald Little Person named Dexter won the first prize Blue Ribbon for sculpture! It carried a $250 award. Since Debbie and Xavier had barely had enough money for gas to get to Kissimmee, the money was a godsend. But the acclaim from experts meant much more to Xavier. It was proof positive he had a quality product. Now he almost had the confidence to risk everything, devote the total of his considerable energies, on his Little People.

The Blue Ribbon was quite an achievement, for two reasons. First, Xavier was a newcomer, going up against competitors much older and vastly more experienced. He could expect no favoritism from judges whose decision would inevitably be tinged by subjectivism. Second, and more significantly, there was the question of whether "soft sculpture" was a legitimate form of sculpture. Terms like "rag doll" and "stuffed sack" were bandied about. When Xavier's Dexter was named as the winner, there was a storm of protest from other artists. The judges stood firm.

Xavier's award for quilting, while gratifying, was not what he had come to Kissimmee to win. Quilts take a long time to produce, and, though they are gorgeous creations, there really isn't the possibility of a mass market, the big score which Xavier was aiming at. Besides, he could never be as skilled as Eula (who, incidentally, would receive some late-arriving acclaim of her own: one of her quilts was featured in *House Beautiful*).

(Also incidentally, Dexter, the Blue Ribbon baby, has occupied a special place of distinction at Babyland General Hospital ever since its opening.)

November, 1977, marked the first significant story that appeared on the Little People. It was published in *Brown's Guide to Georgia*. Xavier mustered his usual flare in talking about his Kids. "Every child is an individual, so we try to find the right clothes and shoes to fit each one's personality. We buy some from garage sales, but some of the children won't wear used clothes, so we have to buy them new ones."

Early in 1978 Xavier developed a uniform pattern by which the babies could be made, making them easier and less expensive to produce. Between February 17-19, at Unicoi State Park's Fireside Craft Show, an annual local extravaganza, he adopted out sixty babies at an average cost of more than forty dollars each.

Nonetheless, Debbie Moreland decided it was time to leave. She was discouraged, Xavier thinks, by the fact that her paintings did not receive the attention the Little People did, and because she was exhausted by the hectic, grueling schedule. Debbie returned to her home in Westminster, South Carolina, not knowing she had been one of the chief witnesses to the beginnings of a genuine American phenomenon.

Xavier was anything but discouraged. Where traveling tired Debbie, it seemed to infuse Xavier with fresh jolts of energy. Days were never long enough for him. And he had the best of all possible worlds. He enjoyed what he was doing and was utterly convinced it would lead to big financial success. As always, Eula thought so too.

Had Xavier known the long odds he faced, been confronted with the laws of probability, the sheer indifference of fate, he might have been less sure of himself, which in turn might have dampened his enthusiasm to try at all. In this respect, a little knowledge is not dangerous; indeed it may be a major reason why certain notable accomplishments are even possible to begin with. No one was around, whispering in Xavier's ear, telling him that grown-up people shouldn't play with dolls, that mountain boys weren't meant to be rich.

Xavier quit his job at the Unicoi State Park craft shop in March, 1978, to spend full-time on his Little People. He continued to make the dolls himself, and to travel the Southeast to display his creations at craft shows. His message never varied: "People of all ages respond to make-believe. If you pretend a baby is real and say he likes peanut-butter cups or is scared of dogs, a child takes it up, and pretty soon the baby has a complete personality."

On July 7, 1978, twenty-two years old, convinced that a whole world waited to adopt his Little People, Xavier convened an unlikely gathering of four young women and one young man; he knew them from school, and asked them to help him with the corporation he intended to form.

• 3 •

Beyond the Georgia Mountains

The group Xavier Roberts brought together on July 7, 1978, to form his company, conventional wisdom would have held, could not have been a less likely collection to succeed in business. There were five of them, all school friends, all inexperienced, all young: Terry Blackwell, the only male, Carol Blackwell, Linda Allen, Sharon Payne, and Paula Osborne. In lieu of wages or salary, which Xavier could not afford to pay, he promised each one five percent of the nascent corporation. The company didn't even have a name, much less an address to do business from, and none of them really had a fixed idea on how to run such an enterprise.

What the five people and Xavier did have was unbounded enthusiasm and energy. They lacked the realization that they *weren't supposed to succeed.* More important, they viewed their work more as fun than as a job; they were underdogs bucking the odds. "We were successful for a number of reasons," says Linda Allen. "First, Xavier had the dream he could do it. Any time one of us would get down, another one would pick us up. No one was ever down at the same time. And we worked at a fast pace, constantly looking to the future."

Not only a fast pace, but a long and tiring one. Yet, they made the job seem fun, which made it bearable, and there was no shortage of energy. And it helped that there really wasn't a boss to oversee it all. The work was easier because they wanted to do it.

The first order of business was to get a place of business —

the Babyland General Hospital, specifically, which Xavier had already listed on those first birth certificates. An ideal place came to mind right away: the Neal Clinic on Underwood Street in Cleveland. The old Neal clinic, personal domain of Dr. L.G. Neal, had been the place where most White County women went to have their babies.

Dr. L.G. Neal had come to Cleveland in 1919, just having been licensed to practice medicine, and built a clinic, with a house next door, on a street which formerly had been a major thoroughfare for Gold Rushers. For forty-seven years, until 1966, he practiced medicine at the same location; two-thirds of all the children in the county during this time were delivered personally by Dr. Neal either at the clinic or at the mother's home. The Neal Clinic more resembled a house than a medical facility, for many White Countians the only one they would ever know.

The overweight Dr. Neal fit the definition of "good country doctor" perfectly: calm, patient, competent, understanding, quietly assured, a man to be counted on in time of need. When a patient calling at his clinic needed additional attention, he would occasionally be housed overnight in Dr. Neal's adjoining home, which was made to double as a hospital. A modern maternity ward was added to the clinic in the 1950s.

The good doctor died in 1969, three years after his retirement, and it seemed that all of Cleveland came out to pay its respects. The clinic was closed and left exactly as it had been. It was sort of a memorial to Dr. Neal and almost half-a-century of medical service; but over the next ten years it fell into disrepair. It was this eventuality which presented the opportunistic Xavier with his idea.

The young dollmaker approached Dr. Neal's daughter. He proposed that his group be allowed to use the clinic in return for repairing and restoring it, and a deal was struck. Thus, the struggling Xavier had a business address, at no cost other than materials and a willingness to work hard, an Anglo-Saxon ethic with which he was bountifully imbued. He was always prepared to work hard.

Xavier, willing to extend any amount of labor to succeed, does not value his time lightly. Here is a man with a purpose.

"I just want to talk to you," he was told, when he was twenty-eight, by an individual who sought information only Xavier could supply.

"How much do I get?" Xavier replied.

"What do you mean? "

"How much money do I get? I worked hard to accomplish what I have. Real hard. And it took twenty-eight years. What I've learned through that hard work I should get paid for."

Xavier, proclaiming to aim for billionaire status, a veritable Mount Olympus where only the gods of industry and their inheritors breathe the rarefied atmosphere, never doubted that his long and fruitful labors had done anything more than confer on him a just and richly deserved reward. Nor would any good have come from mentioning that other men had worked just as hard, and much longer than twenty-eight years (it seemed to sound like twenty-eight hundred coming from his lips), yet they had not been so royally blessed. Xavier had never wondered whether he would succeed: I have to escape poverty, therefore I will. It was a given, and such logic eliminates any consideration of luck.

The problem at the beginning was not with renovating the Neal Clinic, a substantial undertaking that might have discouraged others of less hearty bent. Xavier was good with his hands, loved to work with them to "create something," had learned carpentry from his brothers. Terry Blackwell and the young women possessed skills which melded with one another's; and what four of them couldn't do, the fifth inevitably could. It was enjoyable that summer fixing up the old place, bringing it back to life, fantasy dancing with fantasy — the fantasy they would succeed, the fantasy they were creating a place where babies would be born, not as Dr. Neal had delivered them, but from a cabbage patch.

The difficulty was in not knowing the most rudimentary steps that needed to be taken to start a business. The simplest procedures were foreign to them. Bookkeeping. Accounting. Accounts receivable and payable. Taxes. Government forms. All seemed problems of Gordian knot proportions, and just as hard to unravel.

As Xavier states, "What could I possibly have known about that subject? Nothing. I had no idea how to do it. I'd spend days spinning my wheels, running around, here and there, everywhere. A simple phone call or a postage stamp would have solved the problem, but I didn't know that. I didn't know who to write or who to call."

Meanwhile, the outside of the Neal Clinic was being spruced up, and the inside front room was quickly being converted into a spiffy nursery and maternity ward. The back rooms contained delivery facilities and offices for doctors and nurses. In reality, what was created was a combination gift shop, factory, and home office headquarters, although calling it a gift shop does it a disservice. Then, as even more so today, the place was a children's wonderland, a delight of a little store with dolls everywhere set up in pleasing, attractive, lifelike displays. As word spread, prospective "parents" would travel hundreds of miles to visit the facility. It didn't hurt a bit that aficionados considered the "babies" to be good investments.

"The humanization of the dolls," wrote the *Dallas Morning News*, "is what got them going in the first place. Artist Xavier Roberts, who first came out with the dolls and later authorized Coleco to mass market them, even carried it to the point of putting out almost unbearably sweet little newsletters about fictitious activities of the prototype dolls and formed clubs out of his Georgia-based 'Babyland General Hospital.'"

It wasn't just the humanization. The dolls were arguably works of art, at least those who adopted them thought so. The "fictitious activities" involved baseball games featuring a black Hank Aaron-type slugger (Tyler Bo), a camping enthusiast (Xavier's own Otis Lee), a skier (Sybil Sadie), a tennis star (Amy Loretta), and a struggling preschool student who loves vanilla ice cream (Plain Jane).

Nor was Xavier damaged by having one of his creations in the White House. Much later, First Lady Nancy Reagan would give two Cabbage Patch Kids to South Korean children, and it would generate a flurry of media comment. But this was just icing on the cake during the height of the phenomenon. More important, during the early start-up days, was having Amy Carter frequently being photographed clutching her Little Person.

Xavier thinks success might have come even earlier had he

not had to learn every aspect of business from scratch. "If you have money," he says, "you don't have a problem. You hire an expert and he handles the details for you. But we didn't have any money. That's the way it is with most people who want to go into business."

It wasn't long before Xavier was introduced to the curious habits of bankers, who are often accused of only loaning money to applicants who don't need it. "I'm from a family," says Xavier, "used to working by the hour, twelve hours a day. The townspeople couldn't believe that a hospital for soft sculpture babies would be successful. The banks couldn't believe it either. We got one small loan by putting our personal cars up for collateral, but mostly we had to do business with plastic — a Visa card. With that, I could order up to $700 worth of fabric, thread, and stuffing a month, and there were times we couldn't have kept going if it hadn't been for my mother's quilts. Whenever the pinch got bad she would sell a quilt and give me the money.

"We were a bunch of kids. We didn't know we couldn't do it. We went without lunches and paychecks for a long time. But we imagined how big it would be one day."

Psychologists would undoubtedly find it interesting that so many of the key people in Xavier's life were women. First his sisters, caring for him while their mother worked, then Debbie Morehead, traveling with him to endless craft shows and flea markets and yard sales, then his four women school friends — Linda Allen, Sharon Payne, Paula Osborne, Carol Blackwell — and of course Eula.

The Cleveland citizenry watched with amused interest as work proceeded on the renovation of the Neal Clinic. Rooms were beginning to fill up with cribs, high chairs, rocking chairs, playpens, bassinets, and even an ancient hospital-issue Isolette. These items were acquired much as Xavier had obtained clothes for his first dolls, at yard sales or flea markets, or as hand-me-downs that nobody wanted. People in Cleveland viewed the goings-on mostly with tolerant good humor, amused skepticism, though a few individuals expressed the opinion that the young people were wasting time better spent on more sensibly productive pursuits. None, save Xavier and his mother, and possibly Xavier's minority partners, could imagine the result would be the largest selling first-year doll in history, with toy stores in the United States virtually under seige. Certainly the cynics among Cleveland's population did not have the prescience to realize that Xavier would soon be the town's number one employer, and thus a force to be reckoned with on the local scene.

It was fun for Xavier and his partners to indulge in their fantasy. They even came up with a "Glossary of Terms," tongue-in-cheek but nonetheless something to which they wanted people to adhere.

Doll: "Little People Babies are most certainly *not* dolls, and will tell you so themselves every chance they get."

For Sale: "You cannot buy a Little Person any more than you can buy love or affection. They are, however, available for adoption to good homes."

Shop or Store: "Little People Babies are unavailable in any mere shop or store. They are, though, waiting to be adopted at all Official Adoption Agencies or Placement Centers."

Sales Clerk: "Friendly Adoption Agents or Placement Officers."

Sale: "Better known as an adoption."

Toy: "Little People Soft Sculpture Babies are not toys. They are individually conceived, unique works of art; lovingly hand-crafted collector's items, each with a distinct personality and disposition."

Customers: "There are no customers, only prospective adoptive parents interested in providing good and loving homes for all Little People."

Expensive: "Little People Soft Sculpture Babies are unique works of art; a viable means of investment. Taken over the span of a few years, the cost of adopting one or more is really very little."

Layaway: "Often referred to as an 'adoption option.'"

Place Where Little People Are Made: "Little People Babies are 'born' in the magical Cabbage Patch."

Shipment: "Delivery of the Little People is usually made by the Babyland General Staff Stork — with a little help from his friends at UPS."

Ugly: "Little People have feelings just like anyone else, and are easily hurt, particularly if they are called 'ugly.' "
Imagicillin: "A magical panacea administered to both Little People and adoptive parents in large doses. Guaranteed to cure all variations of the doldrums."

Some of the fantasy had shrewd, hard dollars-and-cents reasoning behind it: "Every baby that leaves Babyland General Hospital has a distinct personality and unique appearance. That is why it is not Babyland General's policy to accept or exchange babies for a seeming lack of asthetic appeal. After all, would you have wanted your parents to have sent you back because they did not like the way you looked?"

It took until September, 1978, to incorporate the operation, a delay undoubtedly occasioned by Xavier's lack of expertise and money. The company was (and is) known as Original Appalachian Artworks, Inc., and its incorporation caused no stir whatever on Wall Street or anywhere else for that matter. Had stock been available, with the company's assets virtually zero, a farsighted investor could have made a killing. But no one was interested. As it was, it took tremendous effort just to purchase fabric and thread.

Also in September a second Blue Edition (the first had listed Helen, Georgia, as the place of birth, and Debbie Morehead as "mother") was released, consisting of a thousand babies. Their birthplace was listed as Babyland General Hospital, Cleveland, Georgia, which indeed, unlike the first edition, was where they really had been made. Collectors can identify them by the prefix "A" in the registration number. Bald babies adopted for $45, girls with hair for $60, boys with hair for $75, and all standing dolls for $125 (no more of these were produced until 1982). Assuming the average adoption fee to be $60, Xavier and his friends were sitting on $60,000 worth of merchandise. If it could be sold.

Survival literally was measured in terms of nickles and dimes. Xavier, charging up to the monthly $700 maximum on his Visa card, tried to get more credit and failed. The time came when he couldn't meet the charges on the Visa card and it was revoked. Always Eula was willing to step in with a

business-saving injection of capital, selling one of her
beautiful quilts, and the meager proceeds purchased more of
the precious material.

In this game it was necessary to stay ahead. It was not
enough to sell what was on hand, something had to be there to
replace the merchandise, and money always seemed to be going out faster than it came in.

Once Babyland General had been renovated, Xavier and
perhaps one of his friends might have made a comfortable living from the business. He had earned himself a local reputa-
tion as the producer of a quality product, and people would
buy from him. But there was no way at this time that the gift
shop-*cum*-factory could support six of them. At any rate, that
wasn't what Xavier aspired to. He wanted to be rich, richer
than any dollmaker before him, and that required reaching
beyond the Georgia mountains.

Xavier was like a man at a craps table hoping he held hot
dice. There was nothing in his past to discourage him.
Wherever he'd shown his babies, they had been popular; he
sensed correctly that people in all places would be attracted to
his Kids. Thus, in September, just after he was legally incorporated, he made the decision to abandon local craft shows
and exhibit his babies only at national trade and gift shows. It
was a bold move designed not only to break into a vastly
larger, more lucrative market, but to challenge the giants of
the doll industry in their own bailiwick.

"Our first show was in Atlanta," Linda Allen remembers,
"and we saw right off that the other displays looked sterile
compared to the adoption center we set up with cribs, toys,
and high chairs. Xavier had the idea of wearing a white doctor's lab coat, and we girls wore nurse uniforms."

Much of the doll establishment, at least where selling to corporate buyers was concerned, had grown sloppy, staid and
stuffy. It wasn't prepared for a group of eager young
Georgians, barely out of their teens, with a new, creative, eye-
catching approach to marketing. Xavier introduced himself as
"Dr. Roberts" and called each of his women partners "Nurse."
Those not instantly turned off by the silliness, which was
never presented in a silly way, stayed to get caught up in the
fantasy.

The Xavier Roberts Show was always entertaining. He wasn't exactly an old-time medicine man hawking his wares from the back of a wagon, he was too shy and soft spoken for that. Nor was he a carnival huckster promising wonders sublime behind the curtain. But his sales pitch was just as effective. He looked and talked like the mountain boy he was. In a gentle voice he would spin fantastic tales, and even the most sophisticated buyers were captivated by this rural charm.

The buyers could also see the time, care, and effort put into the display, obviously a far cry from the take-it-or-leave-it exhibits of some of the more established companies. Of major significance, they studied a quality product, which at first appeared ugly (people who used this word were reminded that the Little People had fragile sensibilities), but whose appeal and attraction seemed to grow on them the longer they looked.

The major roadblock impeding progress for the young entrepreneurs was, as before, their almost total lack of business knowledge. They were neophytes in an industry with centuries of experience. "Buyers," says Xavier, "would come up to us at the Atlanta Merchandise Mart and say, 'Will you take net ten or net thirty?' We'd say we'll have to get back to you on that. Then we'd go find out what it meant."

An encouraging number of orders were taken at the Atlanta exhibition, and soon Xavier and the young women were traveling all over the country, coast to coast, promoting their Little People. For Xavier these promotional forays were the first experiences he had had traveling considerable distances away from Cleveland, but he didn't spend time seeing the sights. The driven young artist saw mainly the inside of auditoriums, one resembling another, and always there were new buyers with whom to share his Cabbage Patch story. It was like the days in the Volkswagen with Debbie Morehead, except the distances were much greater.

The travel was expensive, so was the rental of the booths, and at first it was hard to tell whether the increased sales justified the escalating expenditures. A computer could have told them, or even a competent bookkeeper, but the efficiency of these tools was not yet apparent to the shareholders of

Original Appalachian Artworks, Inc. Besides, there was no money with which to acquire them.

But help was needed. The operation couldn't survive without it. The orders needed to be filled, which meant people had to be hired and then trained to make the dolls. It wasn't a difficult job to teach — for years homemakers, shut-ins, hobbyists, and individuals with simply a lot of time on their hands had been producing similar creations — but it did require that inexperienced management add another responsibility to a list which already was threatening to overwhelm them.

The one thousand babies in the second Blue Edition were all adopted out in less than two months, and the Red, or "B," Edition was introduced. The footprints of the dolls were printed on the back of the birth certificates of this Red Edition, with the result being less than satisfactory in Xavier's refined estimation. For more than a year afterward Xavier would see to it that all certificates were hand stamped. It was in the middle of this Red Edition that the oath of adoption was first required, another ploy thought up by Xavier that would turn out to be a marketing sensation.

The oath could not always be administered. The Rowe-Manse Emporium in Clifton, New Jersey, for instance, during the height of the 1983 mania, ran advertisements for Cabbage Patch Kids, offering forty dollars for dolls which then cost a little more than twenty dollars in stores. Rowe-Manse then offered the dolls for resale at fifty dollars. So many people demanded that Rowe-Manse readopt the Kids to them that it would have been an invitation to homicide to "waste time" administering the oath. Unruly mobs would not have countenanced the delay. It was likewise at the New Rochelle, New York, Merry Go Round Toy Discount Center, where police had enough trouble maintaining crowd control without delays being caused by an oath of adoption, and at Penny Whistle Toys in New York City, where store manager Zina Glazebrook said, "We could charge one hundred dollars each and still not keep them on the shelves."

A side benefit for Xavier in attending every national gift exhibition he could was the amount of press coverage the Little People received. Reporters assigned to cover the events, ever on the lookout for something different from writing about the

208 millionth Barbie, usually ended up stopping at Xavier's booth. Which reporter could resist a mountain boy in doctor's frock, talking on and on about storks and cabbage patches? Xavier was fresh and different, so were the young women in their white, starched nurse uniforms, and they avoided being outrageous by keeping the proceedings low key.

Original Appalachian Artwork's sales at the national trade exhibitions were chiefly to mom-and-pop gift and toy stores. The big department stores and chains, though their buyers often offered encouragement, were committed to large operations like Ideal and Mattel. These industry giants could be relied upon, through massive advertising and promotion campaigns, to supply dolls and toys which moved quickly in and out of stores.

Shelf space, Xavier was learning, was the staff of life for a manufacturer, and it was in exceedingly short supply. Also, the major stores didn't want to carry a very limited quantity of a product. It wasn't worth their time; it was considered a bother. Limited quantity items were for specialty shops. Through efforts that were almost herculean, Xavier had a thousand babies, a number not even a drop in the bucket to operations like Sears or Penney's. Nor did Xavier have much hope of rapidly attaining a capacity that would persuade the big chains to listen, and banks could not be counted on for help. Incredibly, Eula's quilts were still needed to keep Original Appalachian Artworks from sinking into the depths of red-ink oblivion.

Xavier saw the benefits of establishing a franchise operation, whereby individuals, wanting to go into business for themselves, could set up what were called adoption centers. The idea was popular from the inception and over time grew into an elaborate nationwide network of small business owners. Xavier charged an up-front fee for the right to adopt out his babies, and in return provided the adoption centers with a blizzard of advice on how to market the product. They were told how to get "the press to your door" (one idea was photographing a doll being adopted and sending the picture to the local newspaper), what the "keys to success were" (e.g., props, atmosphere, talking about the dolls as if they were children), and how to attract new customers. Basically Xavier relayed to the adoption centers the same principles that worked for him.

The idea of adoption centers to sell the dolls was really nothing new to the business world. With big department stores largely closed to Xavier, it was simply the next best way to reach a wider market. Numerous entrepreneurs have traveled a similar route, but they either didn't have a "better mousetrap" or didn't recruit properly.

The amount of success an individual experienced in the adoption center business, of course, depended on the quantity and quality of the effort expended. One of those who very early hitched her wagon to Xavier's star was Lynda Miller, who, with her husband Tom, is co-owner of the Etc. Shop in Columbia, South Carolina; they hit a mini-jackpot in the adoption center business. A segment of ABC's "Real People" was filmed at the Etc. Shop, and later Ms. Miller talked about her business, how she got into it and how she was doing.

"I found Xavier at the Atlanta Merchandise Mart," Lynda Miller recalled, "on the twenty-second floor, where you don't normally go to find gift items, and they were up there with the cabbage patch and nursery, and my mother and I walked by and saw the babies and immediately fell in love with them. On first sight, I said, 'Oh, fantastic!' Tom — my husband — was with us, and he said, 'No. Absolutely not.' I said, 'This is different.' But we were a very new store at the time, so we passed Xavier by. That night in my hotel room, however, all I could do was think about these babies. So the next morning, when we went back to the Merchandise Mart, my mother and I conveniently got rid of Tom very quickly, and we headed straight for the nursery. When we got there, Xavier talked to us for five minutes, and that was enough. I said, 'I will take them. I don't care what they cost, or what is involved. I want them.' Five sentences was all it took for him to convince me. It was apparent to me at that time what type of appeal they were going to have. Sure enough, as soon as we got them in, they immediately began adopting out. Before we knew it, we were reordering on them. All in all, it took two — maybe three — shipments to convince Tom that maybe this was something we should continue with. But it is, without a doubt, the most intriguing gift item that I have ever carried. And even though we were in our struggling period at the time, the babies are what helped get us on our feet."

Lynda Miller, running just one adoption center (there are many throughout the United States) in an off-the-beaten-path part of America, says the number of dolls she has sold is "in the thousands." She described the Etc. Shop floor space devoted to the babies. "The nursery area is in a room that measures approximately nine by twelve feet, but there are Little People scattered all over the store. In fact, my major display window is always babies. I change the display at least every four weeks, but the whole window is them."

As Xavier expanded into a variety of related areas, Lynda Miller's sales increased. "Because of the fact that the babies can wear real baby clothes, a customer can go anywhere to outfit them. But with Xavier producing his own designer clothes now, the clothes are just as popular as the babies."

Not every adoption center was as inventive as Lynda Miller's. During Christmas, 1983, with people freezing for hours waiting for a store to open, or getting into fist fights with one another, Cabbage Patch Kids were often available at adoption centers. These were more expensive (the most popular model about $125) than the Coleco version, but price did not seem to be an issue, and they were of much higher quality. People searching for an investment — and this was, at least partially, in the minds of many — probably would have been better off, not to mention safer, to have adopted a doll manufactured by Original Appalachian Artworks. But many customers did not know they were available. The adoption centers had not adequately gotten the word out.

Lynda Miller even made money readopting babies, proving at the least that Xavier's earlier dolls had dramatically increased in value. "I'll tell the person who wants to readopt a baby to put it in the newspaper, or — for a small handling fee — I will put it up for readoption in the shop. I find that the hand-signed editions readopt out at $250, $300, and $450. It's a nice investment for the adopting parent." Ms. Miller was speaking of dolls originally selling for about sixty dollars.

Xavier's suggested retail price to adoption centers represented a healthy markup from wholesale, usually double. A doll that Xavier shipped for, say, a price of $37.50 (plus $1 handling charge) would sell at the center for $75. The adoption fee at Babyland General Hospital was the retail cost, not the price charged the franchise holders.

It didn't all come at once, but Xavier discovered almost as many ways to make money from his babies as if he had been adopting out real ones, and then supplying their cradle-to-grave needs. Besides clothes, there were of course all the playthings children need, and gowns and minks and tuxedos when they grew up (or if you wanted to spoil them young). There was even a price list for "surgery."

Broken ankle	$2.50
Broken toes	$4.00
Fractured hand	$5.00
Knee surgery	$3.00
Redesigned mouth	$3.00
Hair transplant	$3.00
Hair transplant (without hair)	$25.00
Hair transplant (with hair)	$30.00
Sprout a new body	$30.00
Sprout a new arm	$6.00
Sprout a new leg	$8.00
Reattached belly button	$2.00
Cleaning or bathing	$10.00
Reattached arm or leg	$3.00
Broken neck	$2.50
Realigned bottom	$3.00
Stitched-up runs (per inch)	$2.00
Elbow surgery	$3.00
Dimple	$2.00
Freckles	$2.00
Repaint eyes	$5.00

The following notice was given to anyone considering mailing their dolls to Babyland General Hospital: "A $5.00 admittance fee will be charged to cover shipping and handling on all surgeries or cleanings."

As the year 1978 came to a close, Xavier had real cause for optimism. The Red Edition, introduced just the month before, had been entirely spoken for, and a Burgundy Edition was being readied for the new year. The Little People were, as Xavier expected, as popular in New York and San Francisco as at Unicoi State Park. Original Appalachian Artworks was far from out of the woods, and up ahead were close, harrowing brushes with disaster. Still, the just-turned twenty-two-year-old artist had come a much greater distance in a very short time than the residents of Cleveland had ever thought possible.

"Although the concept may be based on fantasy," Xavier says, "the results certainly are not."

It was fantasy. It was also a great deal of silliness. Good-natured, fun silliness. Silliness that sold.

Succeeding Against Great Odds

"Some say the stork brings them," read one of Xavier's promotional pieces, "others say the birds and bees have something to do with it, there is even a report that some babies come from the Sears and Roebuck catalog.

"Forget all the preconceived notions you may have about where babies come from. The REAL story is Kids come from the Cabbage Patch!"

At the beginning of 1979, his company starting its first full year of existence, Xavier saw no reason to let up on what had gotten him this far. Spinning a fantasy, the master mountain storyteller attracted the attention of even experienced buyers, who perhaps had wearied of Madison Avenue-brand hype. Bone-deep they knew Xavier's message addressed the child in all of us. These buyers might not be able to place an order, committed as they were to established toy and doll companies, but they did listen and offered encouragement. Xavier's bread and butter, what would keep him going until he found the way to break into the big time, were small gift shops and individual entrepreneurs willing to establish adoption centers.

Xavier very well could have succeeded traveling this relatively narrower route. He might have become a millionaire of the lower echelons, praised, envied, and admired in Cleveland and surrounding communities. A big fish in a small pond. There might even have been fleeting nods of recognition from the giants of the trade, talking about "the eccentric guy from the Georgia boondocks" who "has done all right for himself." When the toy and doll industry figured out each year who was getting which share of the market — Mattel such-and-such a percentage, Ideal such-and-such a percentage — Xavier would have been listed with thousands of independents under the word "others." That wouldn't be too bad for someone who had come from a dirt-poor family and, except for art, had never shown much promise in school. No, it wouldn't have been too bad. The toy and doll industry, after all, had sales of $10.4 *billion* in 1983.

But Xavier had grander ambitions. He wanted nothing less than to be the "biggest in my field," though he couldn't have known, even in 1979, what that meant. He was twenty-three years old and the secrets of business continued to elude him, despite having made an important step four months before when he was legally incorporated. "I had no idea how products even got into the stores. I mean, I never really thought about how a product I might buy in a shop ever got there."

What ultimately led to Xavier's success was not the mastery of business tactics and intricacies, no matter how important they are. "There was never a time I thought about giving up," he says, "or that the business wouldn't succeed. I am not a pessimist. Even when we came home from a gift show without orders to pay our expenses. It just made me work that much harder."

The first months of 1979 were met with two important advances for Original Appalachian Artworks. First, it was no longer feasible to dress the babies in hand-me-downs, or clothes acquired at yard sales or flea markets. Not only did these sources provide an insufficient supply, but too much time was consumed in locating the clothes. Second, the "C" or Burgundy edition was introduced. This consisted of 5,000 babies (previous editions had been 1,000 or less) which were attired in smart new fashions. They were to be sold for $80-$100. Each was autographed by Xavier.

It was a big gamble, putting out five thousand expensive dolls just four months after going into business, but the thought that he might fail had not occurred to Xavier. It seemed like "fun," he says. The five partners helping him build the company viewed it as "succeeding against great odds."

Xavier did not yet know that all the hard work and enthusiasm in the world might not be enough to overcome cold, harsh economic realities. Perhaps it was best he didn't know that part of his future held some close moments verging on total collapse.

What was particularly enjoyable in the early months of this year was enlarging the fantasy of the cabbage patch. It was as if numerous J.R.R. Tolkiens had set their minds to creating an entirely different world. Nor did the moderate successes bring change. Listen to a history of the company, as written by an employee of the company: "Just a few short years ago, Xavier Roberts — a young designer and artist — fathered an entire new race called the Little People Soft Sculpture Babies. By delving into his bag of imagination and totally immersing himself in fantasy, he discovered an enchanted Cabbage Patch where Little People are spawned. With a twist of the wrist and a spark from a dream, young Roberts brought his babies to life.

"Ingenious enough to know that Little People cannot live alone in a Cabbage Patch, Xavier was faced with the dilemma of finding homes for these youngsters. In his small home town of Cleveland, Georgia, Roberts put out his shingle and opened the doors of Babyland General Hospital."

Regardless of the schmaltz, the 5,000 dolls in the Burgundy edition sold steadily. Actually, they should have created a buying panic, as did their 1983 cousins, the Cabbage Patch Kids. Dolls in the Burgundy edition, selling at $80-$100, are now considered to be worth $900.

Xavier clearly possessed soft sculpture skills, and since this was where the money came from, he concentrated his talents on making dolls. But, as it turned out, he had abilities in other areas also, and eventually, when the business did not consume his every waking hour, he found ways to turn these skills to profit. Xavier was adept at antiquing, quilting, woodworking, weaving, decorating, designing, painting, and photography.

What counted at this point, however, was his talent in sales. It took a minor extrapolation to incorporate promotion and public relations skills. His Babyland General Hospital gift shop was carrying its own weight, but the national gift and trade shows were where the real money was, and he continued to be a fixture at these. "I couldn't really buy anything from him," said a representative of a large department store chain.

"Or should I say adopt? But I always stopped by to see what he was up to. Other manufacturers could have learned from him."

G.I. Joe could fit into a broad category of "dolls," and the way this popular figure is marketed contrasted considerably with the fantasy Xavier was selling. The July, 1982, issue of *Toys, Hobbies, and Crafts* carried the following announcement:

Think military! That's what several leading toy manufacturers hope the American public will do this year — and hopefully beyond. There's no doubt that ushered in along with the current presidential administration has been a resurgence of demonstrative patriotism and a renewed interest in the US armed forces. Coupled with escalating international tensions, it's difficult indeed to get through even a single day without at least one thought of armed conflict. Children, too, are exposed on an almost daily basis to military stimuli — in the form of TV news, recruitment ads, classroom studies, movies, and comics, to name just a few sources. Given this new military consciousness, it seems only natural that leading toy companies are putting renewed energy into military-related toy lines.

By way of contrast a typical ad for Cabbage Patch Kids read as follows: "You Can't Buy Love. But You Can Adopt it."

Of equal importance, Xavier was beginning to have his work exhibited in galleries across the United States, including the High Museum of Art in Atlanta. These weren't honors you could pay bills with, but they did help convince early buyers that what they purchased were items of quality. Later, three Cabbage Patch Kids were presented to Georgia Governor George Busbee for inclusion in the state's permanent art collection.

"I didn't consider myself a doll maker," Xavier reflects on his early months in business. "I thought of myself as a life sculptor."

Xavier enjoys talking about how he would get prospective customers interested in his dolls, a talent he still possesses when he chooses to use it. "I'd say she's red-haired. She's short-tempered. Or she doesn't like cookies. They'd carry on with me and pretty soon they'd adopt one. Then they'd send me letters afterward about how the baby's doing."

Xavier lived in a mobile home. Living in fancier quarters, for the present, would have required a financial outlay that better could be used for the business. He'd been in humble housing all his life, and a little longer wasn't going to matter. But, he no longer considered the individual in Cleveland "with the brick house" to be the ultimate possessor of material wealth. When Xavier finally got around to selecting his own residence, it was on a scale of magnitude that would have impressed the most brazen acquisitor.

Xavier's sisters, Barbara and Vivian, and the ever-supportive Eula, were regular sights around the new Babyland General Hospital. They trimmed hedges, landscaped the lawn, planted flowers, helping to turn the gift shop into a pleasant place where people wanted to stop and browse. Later, at the fairy tale house Xavier purchased, her son richer even beyond her own dreams for him, Eula could often be found up to her knees in mud making things grow, "making things nice for Xavier."

"It's a good environment here," a proud Xavier told a visitor to Babyland General Hospital. Then he stopped and smiled, as though thinking of a private joke. "We're all crazy," he said.

On July 4, 1979, Xavier adopted one of his own babies, Otis Lee, dutifully taking the oath of adoption and promising to take care of the Little Person. Otis Lee "just stood out in the crowd," says Xavier. "He looked sort of homely, like he needed a home." Xavier's adopted baby was destined to achieve a certain fame. He would run for president.

Actually, though he started out poor, Otis Lee would travel almost as much as a president. As Xavier's fame spread, Otis Lee accompanied his creator all over the U.S. and to numerous foreign countries. Often he was photographed in a Rolls Royce or wearing expensive clothes. Ultimately he became the unofficial leader of the Cabbage Patch Kids, being right in the arms, as it were, of the father of all of them. Real children wrote to Otis Lee for advice.

One thing not lacking at Original Appalachian Artworks is imagination. Soon Otis Lee was chairman of the board of Babyland General Hospital. A TV series was planned, featuring the Cabbage Patch Kids, starring Otis Lee. Maintaining a straight face, Xavier, talking about his adopted baby, gave the following interview:

Q: How did Otis Lee achieve his position of Chairman of the Board at Babyland General Hospital at such an early age? Does he have a lot of talent, or was he just lucky?

A: No, I think he has a lot of talent. Not only that, but he is a hard worker when he wants to be, and he comes up with a lot of good ideas.

Q: What are some of the places where you and Otis have traveled together?

A: Hollywood was his favorite place. He loved sticking his feet in those of Shirley Temple at the Chinese Theatre in Hollywood. Otis kept insisting that someday his footprints would be there, too, but I think he was just exaggerating. He also liked Aspen and San Francisco. He enjoys doing a lot of skiing. That and going to football games. He's a big fan of the University of Georgia.

Q: Otis Lee is obviously a very eligible bachelor. Has he ever considered the prospects of marriage?

A: He has, but right now things are changing so fast that I don't think it will happen anytime soon. He still has a lot of growing up to do, but don't tell him I said that.

Q: Does he entertain many girl friends?

A: Oh yes, quite often. He loves to take them riding in his limousine. That's his favorite date.

Q: Does Otis ever get embarrassed by all the attention he receives, or does he enjoy being a celebrity?

A: Well, he's basically very shy, and it's sometimes been difficult for him to cope with it all, but I think he's done quite well. Down deep, though, he loves the attention.

Q: Otis Lee has a lot of responsibilities around Babyland. What exactly are some of his duties?

A: He spends a lot of time just making sure that the rest of us are doing things right. He takes a personal interest in seeing that the babies are adopted into good, loving homes. Then there is the mail. He receives — literally — a ton of mail, and he tries to answer it all by himself. He really loves to get mail.

Q: Does he ever wish he could just go away for awhile and do something on his own?

A: Oh, yeah, he's been known to play hookey from time to time. It's hard for him to go to school and do his homework and things like that, because he'd rather be off playing.

Q: What, if any, are Otis Lee's faults?

A: He tends to tell tall tales. He has a very vivid imagination, and sometimes things just get out of hand. He's also the Cabbage Patch ringleader, occasionally getting some of the other Little People into all sorts of trouble. At least they always blame it on Otis.

Q: What does he like to do in his spare time?

A: Well, he likes to plop down in front of the television occasionally and watch his favorite show: The Muppets. He never misses them. Otis also likes to go skiing, and sailing, and he positively loves to go to the movies. In fact, that's the only time that he really keeps quiet, at the movies. Then there is his pet alligator — whose name is Izod — which Otis takes care of.

Q: What is the most personal thing you can tell us about Otis?

A: Probably that he sleeps in an all-blue bedroom, to match his eyes. That's pretty personal. Blue is his favorite color. He also likes to save all the newspaper articles he has appeared in, and put them in a scrap-book which he looks through from time to time. He doesn't really like people to know that, though.

Q: While Otis isn't what you would actually call fat, he certainly looks well-fed. What is his favorite kind of food?

A: Let me say this: there is only one type of food that Otis really doesn't like, and that's cabbage. He definitely hates cabbage, no matter how you fix it.

Q: Xavier, everyone knows that your birthday is on Hallo-ween. But what day is Otis' birthday?

A: Otis was born on the Fourth of July and, frankly, I think that's where he gets his explosive personality from. Really, though, he is very patriotic. But his favorite holiday is Halloween, not because it also hap-pens to be my birthday, but because he loves dressing up in different costumes. One year he put on eleven different costumes, all in the same night.

Q: While you and Otis seem to get along well together, do you ever have any problems?

A: Oh, yeah, we have differences of opinion sometimes. He gets a little spoiled from all the attention and thinks he doesn't have to do things he doesn't like. But everybody occasionally has to do things they don't like, and he's no different. He's still a child, though, and he has some more growing up to do.

Q: What do you think the future holds for the both of you?

A: It seems like the Cabbage Patch is getting bigger and bigger, and there is always more to be done. You'll be seeing a lot more of Otis. He's working now on a line of greeting cards, on books, and on just supervising the overall growth of the Cabbage Patch.

Q: Will Otis ever write his own memoirs?

A: I'm sure. If one book could hold it all.

Otis Lee was called an eligible bachelor, but it wasn't long before Xavier was considered in the same light. In 1983, the International Bachelor Women's Society named Xavier as one of the ten most eligible bachelors in the world. Besides the Cabbage Patch creator, the women's group named Johnny Carson, Boy George, Mr. T., John F. Kennedy, Jr., Dudley Moore, Eddie Murphy, Pierre Trudeau, Gregory Harrison, and Jon Peters. The women's group then went further: they paired each man with an "ideal bachelor girl."

Johnny Carson and Joan Collins. A newspaper commented that "Joan is successful in her own right, so she wouldn't ask for millions (as his last wife did) should the relationship sour."

Boy George and Olivia Newton-John. "Olivia is a fresh-faced outdoor beauty who loves jeans and pants, so Boy George could happily wear the dresses and makeup, without upstaging his lady — a match made in heaven."

Other pairings were Mr. T. and Vanessa Williams, the 1983 Miss America; John F. Kennedy, Jr., and Brooke Shields, "both Ivy Leaguers"; comedian Eddie Murphy and Diana Ross, with Murphy, 22, able to "give new meaning to 39-year-old Diana's old hit *Baby Love*"; Pierre Trudeau and Barbara Walters; Gregory Harrison and Genie Francis; Dudley Moore and Susan Anton; and Jon Peters and Victoria Principal.

Here is what was written about Xavier's matchup with his "ideal" mate, Linda Evans.

Artist-entrepreneur Xavier Roberts, 28, who dreamed up the smash-hit Cabbage Patch dolls, is the man for elegant, cool, Linda Evans of TV's *Dynasty*. For the last 18 months, 40-year-old Linda has let it be known she'd love to have children.

And with Xavier, she could inherit thousands
of little Cabbage Patch Kids with their
adoption papers and cute smiles.

While Cabbage Patch mastermind Roberts is
a good-looking hunk, he needs someone like
Linda to give him style and glamour, to
smooth off the rough edges.

In 1979, Xavier wasn't really seriously considering marriage.
He was too busy trying not just to keep his business function-
ing, but to turn it into an eye-popping success. "I don't know if
I could have found anyone at that time," he says, "who would
have wanted to keep up with me."

Of the five young people who joined Xavier in forming
Original Appalachian Artworks, only Linda Allen did not go
to White County High School. She was a journalism graduate
of the University of Georgia, the only college graduate among
the five, and she did the early, highly successful public relations work that first got the Little People into the public eye.
She helped create the entire present-day world of the Cabbage
Patch Kids, blending skillful writing with large helpings of
fantasy. Linda Allen still holds her five percent of the stock in
the ultra-profitable company, though she no longer takes an
active role in its day-by-day operation. She is studying to
become a television journalist at a school run by the Christian
Broadcasting Network.

Sharon Payne, in the hectic start-up period, was most
valuable in the office and in administration. These were sorely
needed skills. Xavier would have foundered where bookkeeping and recordkeeping were concerned. He was both artist and
salesman, a young man with a vision of riches. Conditions
within the burgeoning business would certainly have
degenerated with him in charge of maintaining a dignified,
businesslike order. Sharon Payne left Original Appalachian
Artworks on December 31, 1980, selling back her five percent
share, to open a gift shop business of her own.

Paula L. Osborne started in production, went to wholesale
selling, returned to take charge of production, and today is
president of the company. The young woman who shared

Xavier's dream is the person to go to if you want to discuss business.

Carol Blackwell, Xavier's first cousin, besides being a hard worker, is resourceful, and she added the first important asset to the fledgling doll-making company. She owned a sewing machine! It was nothing fancy; a similar type could be found in millions of American homes. But it was a godsend to Original Appalachian Artworks. It speeded up manufacture, an absolute necessity if the company were to experience any sort of growth at all. The fact that a home-model sewing machine was essential to the operation illustrates clearly the sort of shoestring operation upon which Xavier had to build. Carol Blackwell maintains her five percent interest in the company, though she also is no longer active in its operation. She has two children who need her attention.

Terry Blackwell, Carol's husband, the only man among the five recruited by Xavier to start the company, was looking for work when presented with his opportunity. He took it without hesitation. A big man, 6'4" and strong, he was able to use his strength to screw what are called "head balls" into the bodies of the dolls. He also provided needed muscle in other areas. Terry Blackwell started in production, and today is in charge of Original Appalachian Artworks' plant, which by far is the largest employer in Cleveland.

In August, 1979, Xavier's work force — "doctors" and "nurses" — numbered fifty-six. Still the company could not keep up with demand. At trade shows and other exhibitions Xavier continued to take more orders than he could fill. Babyland General Hospital itself was a thriving business, attracting people from farther and farther away, but the bulk of the babies were being adopted at an ever-increasing number of centers throughout the U.S. It was impossible for Xavier to predict where it would all lead, or even if the operation would survive. It might all come tumbling down around his ears. It had been difficult enough being his own boss at Unicoi State Park, but now fifty-six others depended upon him. The worst part was having nothing against which to measure himself, no experience with which to compare. He was flying by the seat of his pants learning as he went. It took no tricky calculations to realize he would be all right as long as orders poured in; but what would happen if they started to dry up?

August, 1979, witnessed the introduction of the 'D" or Purple Edition, 10,000 babies in all. Xavier signed each one. These dolls, adopting for $80-$100, are today estimated to be worth $750 each. The Purple Edition consisted of twice as many dolls as any previous offering, but there seemed no problem finding homes for them. In fact, production facilities were immediately cranked up for a new offering.

Even this early in the game, increasing numbers of people were buying the dolls as investments. Xavier wasn't averse to selling them as such, but he admitted his knowledge of the collectibles market was limited. "I really don't understand it," he said. "People seem to just go crazy and are willing to pay any price. Then they resell them and mark them up even more. All of a sudden the Little People are going for thousands of dollars."

Actually, only the Helen Blue, "A" Blue, and "B" Red climbed to more than $1,000, but numerous others pushed that mark. Why did Xavier believe the dolls appreciated in value? "I think the public finds them really unique. And uniquely American."

Unique they were. It was the fact that each *was* different, not produced from the same cookie cutter, that so many buyers found them attractive. Xavier knew this. He wondered, if sales ever soared into the millions, as he hoped, how each could remain a one-of-a-kind. In this respect he would turn out to be in perfect step with technology. Computerization was making one-of-a-kind goods a mass-produced reality.

The big problem was knowing how many dolls to produce. What if Xavier made too many, and ended up stuck with them? This had been the fate of countless manufacturers in every conceivable industry down through the ages. The curse of over-production. Over-production has caused national and worldwide depressions. It could surely sink a Cleveland, Georgia, doll-maker with no financial cushion, no resiliency to help him wait out a slack period and bounce back. Yet in the autumn of 1979 Xavier went ahead with plans for his biggest edition yet, 15,000 babies in all. In actuality, there loomed a harrowing test that would threaten to sink them all, but none of the young Georgians was thinking failure at this time.

Far Left: (Above) The Cabbage Patch Kids enjoy a popularity oversees. Hectic buying at Hanley's toy shop on London's Regent Street. Christmas 1983. (Below) Male employees of Tokyo's *Takashimaya* Department Store line up to regulate the flow of prospective Cabbage Patch customers. February 1984.
Left: Edward Pennington, unable to find his daughter a Kid in the US, flew to London to get them. (Below) Even Cartier's in Beverly Hills had their own, specially-made Kid — draped in jewels, of course.

(AP/Wide World)

The Most Sought After Gift

(Above) Dolls delivered by armored car in New Britain, Connecticut, are sold within ten minutes of their delivery. (Below) Rather than risk having their store ransacked, one store gave their Kids to hospitalized children. *Far Right:* A Cabbage Patch auction in Minnesota nets $8,000 for charity. (Dottom) Xavier Roberts unveils Coleco's 1984 line of Cabbage Patch characters in New York.

(AP/Wide World)

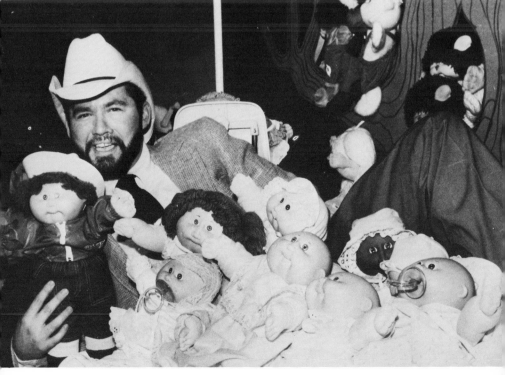

(Above) Xavier as a child. Xavier's mother and
father, Eula and Happy.
At a Roberts' family reunion, the young Xavier dons
his Indian headress.
Far Right: Dexter, one of the earliest of the Little
People, won a blue ribbon for sculpture at the
Osceola Art Show in Kissimmee, Florida.

The Little People

a tare - Xavier

soft sculptures

DEXTER

Limited Signed Edition

Johnson's
baby
powder

PUREST PROTECTION

Johnson

Examples of Xavier's early work in quilting and soft sculpture. (Below) "Face in a hat."

Xavier Roberts

Babyland General, before and after renovation. Dr. Neal stands in the walkway to the old clinic.

Much of the success of Babyland could be attributed to the life-like situations Xavier created for his Kids.

Some members of the staff at Babyland. They are referred to as "doctors" and "nurses."

(Above) A Cabbage Patch Birth. The "parents" look in on the operation.
(Right) The Cabbage Patch playland, Another World.

(Overleaf) What started out on a shoestring
and a prayer, with a staff of 5, has now
developed into a sizeable operation for a
town the size of Cleveland, Georgia.
(Above) Xavier Roberts adopts Otis Lee as
his own special Little Person. Otis Lee
figures to play a prominent role in Xavier's
growing fantasy.

Meantime, there were more amusing incidents than financial cliffhangers. A major department store buyer remembers
several of Xavier's saleswomen approaching her, dressed as
nurses and carrying a sample baby. "This is nuts," she recalls
saying to herself. "I tried to cordially show them the door.
And even during that first visit, one of our customers saw the
doll and asked if she could buy it on the spot. 'You don't *buy*
this Little Person,' the representative told her. 'You *adopt.*'
'Fine,' the customer said. And would you believe, they went
right out on the sidewalk to take care of their transaction!"

Increasing numbers of newspapers and magazines were
finding Xavier and his babies to be irresistible stories, and the
good publicity helped spur increased demand at this time.
Xavier already had word-of-mouth advertising working for
him, and his own prodigious efforts to meet anyone remotely
interested in his dolls, but a newspaper story could reach tens
of thousands of readers. It was better than any paid ads he
could run, even if he'd had the money to run them. It was not
long before *Dolls, The Collector's Magazine*, took notice. "As art,
these Little People stack up as well-designed and well-crafted
soft-sculpture of unusual charm and originality. Nothing quite
like them has appeared on the doll market. As collectibles,
well, let's put it this way: early editions of Roberts' 'kids' (circa
1978-79) that once sold for $30-$80 are now commanding
prices up to $3,000."

If Xavier professed to know little about the collectibles
market, he claimed no similar ignorance of the appeal he
thought they would have. "I knew people would become attached to them," he says. "I got so attached that if a baby
stayed around too long, I couldn't bear to part with it. If it
wasn't for the money they brought in putting me through college, I would have kept them all. Even today, if I have them
around too long, I can't part with them."

Among the early newspapers to take note of what would
become Cabbage Patch Madness was the *Chicago Tribune*, which
called it a "polyester baby boom." The *Pensacola* (Florida)
News-Journal dismissed individuals who thought the Little
People were unattractive by saying the same individuals
would "also find rainbows and moonlight annoying." *Venture*
magazine noted that Xavier was creating "America's newest
baby boom from an abandoned country hospital in the two-

stoplight town of Cleveland, Georgia, where he has lived all his life."

When you come right down to basics, there are really only two kinds of dolls: play and working. Play dolls, as their name indicates, are made to be played with, while working dolls serve a different function, such as to display fashions or to illustrate an occupation. At first Xavier was quite firm on which group he believed his dolls inhabited. "The Little People aren't toys," he said. "They're collector's items, individual works of art." Perhaps so. But children were encouraged to play with the Little People, to take them wherever they went — to parks, playgrounds, zoos, on camping trips and to ball games.

The 1979 Christmas Edition, denoted by the prefix "X," was introduced in November. There were only one thousand dolls ($150 each) in this offering, but they were special because they had snow white hair and came dressed in red velveteen. They came with an oversized birth certificate, and today are estimated to be worth $750.

But the big edition, the Bronze, 15,000 strong, was released in December, 1979. At an average of $100 a doll, this was $1.5 million in merchandise. A lot of cabbage, as more than one publication pointed out, for a company that had just opened its doors the year before. Today these dolls are estimated to be worth $650 each, a remarkable appreciation in value for an edition that was so large.

The respected *Decorating & Craft Ideas* magazine lent a helping hand by reporting that babies "with bottoms signed by Xavier are expected to become collector's items in a few years."

This sort of publicity had to help. A parent looking for a doll for her daughter (and more than 90% of sales were to adults) could have found something less expensive than the Little People. But the idea that what was being purchased might increase in value put a different light on the matter. Most Americans really couldn't afford to lay out $100 for a doll, but it wasn't really a lot for an item that might be much sought-after in the future.

As 1979 ended, Xavier could look back on a year of almost uninterrupted success. Babyland General Hospital had become a showcase in the Southeast, and people came from hundreds of miles away to take the guided tour, conducted by a freshly-uniformed, fresh-faced "nurse," and to stay long enough to adopt one of the babies. More important, adoption centers were reordering, and new adoption centers were being established all over the country. The pleasant problem facing Xavier, the same one he'd grappled with back in the Unicoi State Park days, was how to keep up with demand.

The demand wasn't just for the dolls. The media wanted to meet Xavier. There were so many requests for interviews that a public relations aide had to be hired to determine which ones Xavier should grant. He literally could have kept busy twenty-four hours a day talking with the press, which at this time would have been a cart-before-the-horse arrangement. Xavier realized that while he was playing pied piper to the press, everything else might disintegrate, and hiring a public relations aide was a hedge against that onerous possibility.

One interview Xavier granted during this time gives a good insight into his thinking. He said he thought his dolls brought out a "parental instinct" in customers, but that he didn't worry about people becoming emotionally attached to them, lost in a fantasy. "They're not really escaping from reality," he said. "When they carry their baby down the street, people stop to ask about them. They enjoy the attention."

Xavier was asked if he thought the appeal of the Little People would last. "I don't know where it is going," he said, "but it has been fun. The people who had a baby last year want another this year. They get more and more attached to them."

"Did you ever," the doll maker was asked, "in your wildest dreams, imagine this would happen?"

Xavier simply replied, "You have to want something badly enough in order to get it. I wanted it."

Helping him get it, particularly in the early years of struggle, before the Cabbage Patch Madness engulfed the nation, was a multitude of individual doll collectors. Not much is printed about these people, but they number in the many scores of thousands in this country. They have discovered there can be money in dolls . . . a great deal of it.

• 5 •

More Than Mere Playthings

While many so-called sensible citizens viewed the Cabbage Patch Madness of 1983 with amusement or dismay — "Look at the crazy people stampeding for a doll," or "Isn't it too bad their values are so mixed up?" — there just might have been some hard, cold, clever financial calculations going on in the minds of some of those who stood in line risking physical harm. We may not know for twenty years or more, when collectors begin bringing out their Cabbage Patch Kid purchases and start testing the market for the worth of the dolls. If the boxes the dolls come in are unopened, and Joanne Donna or Tillie Susan look like they're still waiting to be cuddled, it will be apparent the Kids weren't purchased merely because a daughter or granddaughter wanted a Christmas present.

Consider this: a Barbie that cost $3 in 1959 now sells for as much as $1,000, an astounding increase of more than 33,000%!

Reliable estimates place the number of *serious* doll collectors in the United States at more than 250,000, and the total is growing fast. These people do not fit the popular misconception of the lonely, oddball Bette Davis-type old maid living alone, or the sweet grandmother dressing her dolls for dinner as she lectures kindly about the virtues of table manners. On the contrary, a third of the collectors are men.

One of these was John Wayne, the punch-'em-in-the-nose actor, whose collection of beautifully attired Hopi Indian dolls is part of a display at the National Cowboy Hall of Fame in Oklahoma City. Wayne also was the model for a 1981 doll which came complete with cowboy hat, saddle, and carbine.

Nor are the collectors likely to be dreamy connoisseurs of nostalgia or aging childless women employing dolls as substitutes for the babies they never had. Flinty-eyed members of the investment-oriented Rockefeller family, ever alert for ways to turn a profit, have long been in the habit of collecting dolls.

The Madame Alexander dolls, if discontinued and more than ten years old, can be worth up to $1,000 each. The Mme. Alexander Doll Company of New York has introduced the Scarlett O'Hara doll; the Sonja Henie doll; the Jeannie Walker doll; the Little Genius doll; the Alice in Wonderland doll; and many others. When Madame Alexander issued the Enchanted Doll in 1980, it came with a signed and numbered affidavit that guaranteed the edition would not exceed three thousand. As early as 1977, Xavier, not even incorporated yet, was making a similar promise. Such documents, of course, are invaluable when it comes to protecting an investment.

All Shirley Temple dolls more than twelve years old are valuable. Several of them have brought more than $1,000 each. Peter Playpal dolls that are in good condition are valued at upwards of $500. Almost all celebrity dolls, such as the John Wayne or the Mary Pickford (this one sported the "flapper" look), have a market. Royal Doulton recently issued a $7,400 Marilyn Monroe doll which was dressed in an ermine coat.

One successful collector is Memphis dentist, Thomas O. Nash, who chiefly searches for carved wooden and bisque dolls manufactured in the early 1900s by the Philadelphia firm of A. Schoenhut & Co. Dr. Nash offers the following good advice: "Don't buy junk. You have to get going with the finest pieces."

Not everyone can afford this advice, however, and a number of collectors beat the bushes for flea markets and yard sales. Bargains can be found by the individual aware of what he is doing. Many dolls have sat in an attic for a lifetime (not a good idea — unattended dolls can be damaged by age and deterioration), and their owners, often thinking they are merely clearing away debris, may have no idea of their value. The attraction of browsing through yard sales is the possibility, however slight, of hitting a jackpot, perhaps a Jumeau doll, forgotten all these years, worth $20,000.

Another avid doll collector is Potomac, Maryland, attorney Arnold P. Popkin, who emphasizes the importance of a doll's condition. "Know the difference between a broken finger and a broken head." A broken finger may not be important. A hairline crack through the head can reduce a doll's value by ninety percent.

Probably no doll collector ever matched the late Margaret Woodbury Strong, the largest single stockholder in Eastman Kodak, who died in 1969. Mrs. Strong had 27,000 dolls! She also had 700 dollhouses. Her long-time secretary described her as a "compulsive buyer," presumably an accurate and fair summary. Just as gambling can be compulsive, addictive, so too, experts have pointed out, can doll collecting. It gets in the blood, as most hobbies can. Many marvelous doll collections exist which the owner wouldn't think of selling. Some newspapers scoffed at the claims of buyers who said they "would never part with" one of Xavier's original creations, but the owners may simply have been stating the unvarnished truth. For some people dolls take on a life of their own, becoming part of the family.

Socrates was interested in dolls, and so was William Penn. But the entrance *en masse* of men into the field is a relatively recent development. The phenomena is credited with driving up the price of collectible dolls. Often at auction, as the prices being bid begin to stagger the imagination, it is the men who are most competitive and aggressive.

What can happen when dolls are offered for sale is perhaps best illustrated by what occurred October 16, 1982, when Samuel Pryor gave a few of his more than 8,000 dolls to Sotheby Parke Bernet to auction. Mr. Pryor, a former Pan American World Airways vice president, got started as a doll collector by way of an inheritance. During his travels he had bought numerous dolls for Ann M. Archibald, another Pan Am executive, and when she passed away Pryor discovered that she had willed her collection to him. Pryor began adding to his new collection, until finally he bought a farm and turned its barn into a museum. It drew thousands of visitors to the site, which was near Greenwich, Connecticut, the idly curious as well as serious students of dolls. Pryor decided to place some of the collection on the block, with the proceeds going to charity.

At Sotheby Parke Bernet in New York City, bidders could view the dolls on closed circuit TV. Telephone lines were kept open so bidders as far away as the West Coast could get into the action. It was fast and furious from the beginning.

Three French Bru dolls went for $5,200, $6,500, and $8,500 respectively. These might have cost $75 in 1946, $600 in 1960. Five Italian Lenci dolls were auctioned. A glass-eyed Lenci brought $1,900. Another, holding a jump rope and dressed in a red pinafore, brought $1,500. A doll dressed as a tennis player went for $1,200, a polo player for $1,700, and a golfer for $3,250. The golfer was dressed in knickers and held a golf club.

A doll from Germany, estimated in the Sotheby Parke Bernet catalog to be worth $200-$250, was sold for $2,500. Incredibly, the Sotheby Parke Bernet catalog for the Samuel Pryor auction was immediately judged to be a collectible, and someday it likely will be for sale!

Sybill McFadden, writing in *Hobbies* magazine on the Pryor auction, described the item expected to cause the most excitement. "The Magic Cupboard is a French automaton, Vichy, late 19th century. It has a boy seated on the counter of a cupboard. He turns and reaches toward the cabinet door which opens. A fly appears and 'flies' out of the boy's reach. The psychological twist comes when the boy hesitates upon seeing a pot of his grandmother's gooseberry jam, turns backward and forward, then reaches for the pot, whereupon the pot spins around to show his grandmother's face on the other side with her spectacles rising and her jaw dropping in alarm — his guilty conscience? The boy turns again, gestures with the biscuit in his hand, nods his head, gestures with his right hand, and sticks out his tongue. Finally, as the cupboard door closes, a mouse appears over a red ball of Edam cheese sitting in the counter. The catalogue estimated the cupboard at $8000 to $12000."

It was auctioned for $23,100.

A telephone bidder at the Sotheby Parke Bernet auction paid $6,600 for a French Magician doll. This doll, dressed in a top hat, pulls out a mouse, then — presto! — reveals a cat in its place.

The dolls auctioned by Sotheby Parke Bernet were not the modern variety. It should be noted that prices for old and antique dolls vary in different sections of the United States. They usually command a higher price on the East and West Coasts than in the country's midregion. Two of Xavier's early dolls were auctioned for charity in 1983, and brought $2,500 and $3,000 respectively. But the truth is, a doll is worth exactly what someone is willing to pay for it, and no more. Florence Theriault of Annapolis, Maryland, put one of Xavier's 1978 $250 "works of art" up for auction and the top bid was $160.

Original Appalachian Artworks itself has put together a concerted effort to appeal to collectors. By the company's own estimation, what follows on pages 84 and 85 are how its babies have done in the collectibles market.

Xavier got his start selling limited edition dolls, and as can be seen by the following chart, his earliest creations have skyrocketed in value. But Xavier was far from the first to come up with the idea. The Effanbee Doll Corporation in New York City started a club for collectors in 1975. There was no charge for joining the club, but a member did have to promise to buy one of the 872 Precious Baby dolls that Effanbee put out. These cost $40, and the next year, 1976, the company offered 1,200 Patsy dolls for $35 each. A Precious Baby or a Patsy is currently estimated to be worth between $250 and $300.

Collectors take into consideration five prime factors in determining the value of a doll. First is age. Probably the oldest it is still possible to purchase is the Queen Anne, dolls named for the English monarch who reigned from 1702-1714. The key is knowing whether a doll really is old, or something which is being passed off as such. Like anything else, doll collecting is refined through study, and because the hobby is so popular and potentially lucrative there are numerous books on the subject in almost any library.

The second factor to consider is the condition of the doll. Since a good deal of money is involved, people who collect dolls do not permit them to be used as playthings. Those $1,000 Barbies were still in their original boxes, or according to the *Americana & Collectibles* price guide, they were worth just $500, even if in perfect condition. It is usually best if a doll has not been handled at all. Collectors do not invest in a doll so Junior can rough-house with it, or use it as a substitute football. Those who possess the most valuable of Xavier's earliest creations purchased the dolls and promptly put them out of harm's way. Also, collectors check to see if there is chipping, cracking, peeling, and especially if any parts are missing. Although, as *Business Week* magazine, December 19, 1983, reported, "An extremely rare bisque doll — whose head had been glued back together after it was broken into 20 pieces — was auctioned last year for $8,000," it is far preferable to possess "mint" condition merchandise. Says Annapolis, Maryland, auctioneer, Florence Theriault: "You're way out in left field if you're bent on speculation. If you attempt to resell in two or three years, you'll take a loss. You've got to give a doll more like twenty years to find its market."

Third is rarity. If very few of a particular type of doll are available, the reality of supply and demand enters the picture. This again points out the desirability of staying with dolls where the number in the edition is known to be limited. Almost always a male doll will be more rare than its female counterpart, for the simple reason that more females are produced.

Fourth is the history of the doll. It is best if the doll is part of the history of a particular country, area of the country, or the heritage of a distinguished people. It is better still if the doll was the plaything of someone famous. This is referred to by collectors as a doll's provenance. Just as a desk used by Abraham Lincoln would bring a higher price than an identical desk which belonged to an unknown individual, so too would a doll that is known to have been owned by, say, Queen Victoria. "The fact remains," wrote Catherine Christopher in *The Complete Book of Doll Making & Collecting*, "that, while mute, the doll is highly expressive of a variety of significant factors. More enduring than some of the mightiest monuments ever built, the doll has persisted throughout the ages as an imperishable expression of men's dreams. Unwittingly the doll reveals the tremendous scope of man's endeavors, inventive ingenuity, manufacturing zeal. The doll has portrayed political whims, even national bloodthirstiness, as did the wooden doll which was made during the latter part of the nineteenth century in Vermont expressly for export to Japan. This doll had an ingenious arrangement which allowed the Japanese child to decapitate the doll without destroying it!"

Among dolls having a history are those which were used

EDITION	# In Edition	Original Adoption Fee
"Helen" Blue	Less than 1,000	$30-150
"A" Blue	1,000	$45-125
"B" Red	1,000	$80-100
"C" Burgundy	5,000	$80-100
"D" Purple	10,000	$80-100
"X" 1979 Christmas	1,000	$150
"E" Bronze	15,000	$80-125
"SP" Preemie	5,000	$100
1980 Celebrity	5,000	$200
1980 Christmas	2,500	$200
*Grand Edition	1,000	$1,000
*1981 New 'Ears	15,000	$125
"U" 1980/1981 Unsigned	73,000	$125
*"PR II" Preemie	10,000	$130
*1981 Standing Edition	5,000	$300
*"PE" 1982 New 'Ears Preemie	5,000	$140
"U" 1982 Unsigned	21,000	$125
1982 Christmas	1,000	$200
1982 Cabbage Patch Kid	2,500	$125

CABBAGE PATCH KID EDITIONS:

"Cleveland" Green	2,000	$125
"A" Darker Green	2,000	$125
"B" Red	2,000	$125
*"C" Burgundy	10,000	$130
*"D" Purple	20,000	$130
Oriental	1,000	$150
American Indian	1,000	$150
*Hispanic	1,000	$150
Champagne	2,000	$250
*1983 Christmas	1,000	$200
1984 Sweetheart	1,500	$150
Bavarian	1,000	$150
*World Class	2,500	$150
*"E" Bronze	30,000	$130

*Still being delivered from the Cabbage Patch

Current Estimated Value	Birthmark	Additional Products
$4,000	Signed	Little People Pals
$2,000	Signed	10,000 signed
$1,700	Signed	Original retail:
$1,300	Signed	$75.00
$1,100	Signed	Current Value:
$1,500	Signed	$150/$200
$ 900	Signed	
$ 700	Signed	Debonaire Bear #1
$ 600	Signed	1,000 signed on
$1,000	Signed	cuff.
$1,000	Signed	Original retail:
$ 150	Stamped	$75.00
		Current Value:
$ 250	Stamped	$500.00
$ 150	Stamped	
$ 350	Stamped	Debonaire Bear #2 *
		2,500 printed on
$ 150	Stamped	vest.
$ 200	Stamped	Original retail:
$ 450	Stamped	$75.00
	& Autographed	Current Value
$ 400	Stamped	$75.00
		Wizards *
		2,500 stamped
$ 300	Stamped	Original retail:
$ 150	Stamped	$75.00
$ 150	Stamped	Current Value
$ 130	Stamped	$75.00
$ 130	Stamped	
$ 350	Stamped	Humphrey Furskin *
$ 350	Stamped	2,500 stamped
$ 150	Stamped	Original retail:
$1,000	Signed	$75.00
$ 200	Stamped	Current Value
$ 200	Stamped	$75.00
$ 350	Stamped	
$ 150	Stamped	
$ 130	Stamped	

These Adoption Fees refer to reported
estimated values from collectors and devotees of
Cabbage Patch Kids and Little People Babies.

during the Civil War for smuggling drugs and medicine through Union lines to Confederate soldiers. Some dolls were considered so valuable that ships which carried them were accorded neutrality by nations which were at war.

Fifth and finally is the clothing the doll wears. "Clothing," wrote doll expert Izole Dorgan, "is not just a dress that is becoming to a doll. It should be a bit of fabric contemporary with her, buttons, tapes and all, it should be a garment that when contrasted with later day models, tells a story. A true story." Of course, dolls were used as manikins in the royal courts of Europe, and these were dressed in the highest fashions, complete with hats, gloves, parasols, cashmere shawls, lace, furs, and jewelry.

The collector with good taste can turn a healthy profit buying dolls from free-lance artists, such as Xavier. These artists usually limit their editions to one hundred or less. Xavier's first edition, the "Helen" Blue, which sold for between $30 and $150 in 1977, are estimated now to be worth $2,000. What the Georgia artist was able to cash in on was the superior quality of his product, and the fact that even within given limited editions, each doll was different. The 872 Precious Baby dolls put out by Effanbee were alike. And what Xavier's dolls may have working for them now is a bit of history, the memory of the riots of Christmas, 1983.

But what will be "hot" in the future can at best only be part of an educated guess. As Kyle Husfloen, editor of *The Antique Trader Weekly*, points out, "More people are collecting more things for fun, for profit and simply for the thrill of accumulating." Mr. Husfloen guesses that hot items in the future might include literature about Three Mile Island, Farrah Fawcett dolls, and Six Million Dollar Man dolls. A Nixon campaign button, to stray away from dolls for a moment, is worth about $40.

It cannot be gainsaid that history plays an important factor in doll collecting. A shrewd collector will notice immediately, for example, the size of a china doll's feet and hands. If they are unusually tiny, it is because they come from an unlamented time in that country when women had their feet bound and had to cram them into shoes barely large enough for a baby.

The manufacturers of the Brooke Shields doll and the Michael Jackson doll are hoping that what happened to Barbie in 1959, or the Cabbage Patch Kid in 1983, happens for them in 1984. What they won't have working for them is the uniqueness of each Cabbage Patch Kid, and although a doll can outlive the popularity of the person after whom it is modeled, e.g., the Shirley Temple, it wouldn't hurt if Mr. Jackson and Ms. Shields maintain their celebrity over many years, a questionable prospect.

Beginning doll collectors probably are wiser if they concentrate on a single kind, rather than just dolls in general. It is easier to become expert if the collector's scope is limited, especially in a field where the variety available approaches the infinite. A number of collectors specialize in 19th century white bisque dolls, one of which recently brought a record $38,000 bid at auction. Others are primarily interested in "personality" dolls, such as the Dionne Quintuplet or Shirley Temple models of the 1930s, or dolls manufactured in the 1800s by the Jumeau family of France, many worth up to $20,000 each.

Just as stamp collectors call themselves philatelists, and coin collectors are known as numismatists, many doll collectors refer to themselves as plangonologists. The word comes from the classical Greek *plangon*, meaning doll. And just as stamp and coin collectors often try to specialize (who possibly could be expert at everything ever available?), so also do most astute collectors of dolls. For example, a collector might limit his acquisitions to Pedlar Dolls, first made in the late 18th Century, which are depictions of real-life peddlers offering their wares.

Other collectors might specialize in wax dolls, or unglazed dolls, China Heads, peg wooden dolls, papier maché heads, wax over composition dolls, or any number of varieties. In any event, it is important to know the difference between an original and a reproduction. Often the most simple method is best: a reproduction may look too good to be true. Already there have been fake Cabbage Patch Kids, and in this respect the passing out of birth certificates and adoption papers furnishes at least some indication of genuineness.

Certain givens are known to all serious doll collectors. The head of the doll, for example, is always more important than its body. The value of dolls can change erratically, though in recent years the trend has been upward. Large dolls are generally, but not always, more valuable than small ones, everything else (condition, quality, etc.) being equal. (A large doll, incidentally, is considered to be one 32 inches or more in height.) And closed-mouth dolls are generally considered more desirable than open-mouth dolls, probably because fewer of them were made.

The safest doll, in terms of protecting an investment and not shelling out $20,000 for a Jumeau, may be the portrait or personality type. Thomas Jefferson, Mary Todd Lincoln, George and Martha Washington, and Jacqueline Kennedy Onassis have been favorite subjects of collectors. Also Jayne Mansfield, Cher, Marie Osmond (who adopted a Cabbage Patch Kid), Deanna Durbin, and Jenny Lind, the "Swedish Nightingale."

Along with the collecting of dolls comes the collecting of dolls' houses, and some of these are breathtakingly beautiful. Interestingly, more men than women collect and furnish these houses. Since a doll can be fantasized into having all of the physical needs of a baby (indeed, houses for dolls were first called baby houses), collectors also accumulate doll clothes and accessories. Even dolls to be playmates for dolls. The Cabbage Patch Kids have Pals, for example, which presumably keep them occupied and happy. There are collectors who exercise as much care furnishing a doll house as they do their own, which in truth may be necessary to the investment. If the doll house is from the Georgian period, that style has to be imitated or the look likely will seem ludicrous.

No shortages exist where accessories are involved. Coleco has produced Cabbage Patch "Koosas," which are pets for Cabbage Patch Kids, and "Pin-Ups," miniature Cabbage Patch dolls which Cabbage Patch dolls can hold. *Newsweek* magazine called the Cabbage Patch Kids "anything but child's play."

There are a number of mistakes to avoid if you are a beginning doll collector. It is unwise to inform a seller that you don't know what you're doing, even if you don't. Also, a seller of dolls is not likely to be moved to compassion by the buyer saying he is short of cash. Doll collecting is a luxury. Besides, there are *always* more buyers for a good doll than there are good dolls to go around. John C. Schweitzer, author of *The ABC's of Doll Collecting*, also advises, "Avoid buying a doll whose wig or shoes seem impossible to remove. The seller may be trying to discourage you from locating areas on the doll that have been damaged or restored. One unhappy collector of choice French dolls paid top dollar for a beautiful, marked Bru. When she finally succeeded in removing the shoes, she discovered crude clay stumps, rather than feet! (She returned the doll and fortunately got her money back.)"

But many dolls are sold "as is," and the *caveat emptor* (let the buyer beware) rule usually applies. Before buying a doll it is wise to handle it and inspect it closely. If you're a serious buyer, no seller should object. It is a good idea, however, not to bring children to a sale of expensive dolls. The eyes of sellers spotting Junior playing with their prize Jumeaus will bulge with the same look of shock a maitre d' will have when he catches sight of a vagabond approaching his exclusive, hallowed eatery. These dolls, although playthings in spirit, are not meant to be played with, any more than collector plates are intended to be eaten from.

Also to be avoided, once a collection assumes value, is loose talk about its existence. The theft of doll collections, or individual valuable dolls, has become almost as commonplace as the stealing of jewels.

When selling part or all of a collection of dolls, the atmosphere of the sale can be crucial. The surroundings should be as exciting and lifelike as possible, never drab. "A festive air," wrote Clara Hallard Fawcett twenty years ago in *Dolls, A New Guide for Collectors*, "to the whole exhibition is desirable — lights, color and music help tremendously. A good phonograph is one of the best assets of the amateur show. Festoons of brightly colored crepe paper from the middle of the ceiling to the walls help when flowers and ferns are not available."

Knowing how to exhibit dolls, of course, was Xavier's forte — and what brought him his earliest attention. People were attracted to what he did. Xavier paid close attention to the vital detail of atmosphere while other much more established firms preferred to rest on past successes. An individual planning to exhibit a doll collection, or set up any other display, for that matter, could do worse than emulate the Georgia artist's eye-catching, attention-grabbing methods.

Xavier's ploy of talking about his dolls as if they were real babies was nothing new either, just a going-back-to-basics that had been forgotten by other manufacturers. "Hi, there!" a puppet witch used to greet passersby at a summer camp display. "Want your fortune told? What! You don't believe in such things? Now, by my secret, sacred brew, the things I tell you *will* come true!" This gimmick would bring shoppers to the summer camp display, just as Xavier weaving tales of a preposterous Cabbage Patch attracted people to his booth.

That the Cabbage Patch Kids are collectibles is proved merely by the fact that people collect them. Individuals with a dozen or more are not uncommon, and a few have collections that number in the hundreds. But what will they be worth in the future? It is difficult to say. One thing most collectors do agree upon, Xavier's original creations will probably increase in value, as they become more rare among the millions Coleco anticipates selling. At one time, for example, the Helen Blue edition dolls numbered 1,000 out of, say, three thousand in circulation. Soon they will probably be 1,000 out of tens of millions.

6

A Year of Fanfare

The 15,000 dolls comprising the Bronze Edition, released late in 1979, were selling more briskly than any previous offering, and 1980 did not appear to Xavier to be a year to go bearish. What he had thought all along, in fact, was coming true. People everywhere loved his babies, and the only challenge was how to make them as readily available as popcorn or soap. The ominous inflation rate of Jimmy Carter's last year in the White House seemed light years away from booming Babyland General Hospital. The recession just hadn't gotten around to Xavier yet. His product appealed to a middle-class not yet screaming for mercy. It would arrive, however, as surely as the tax man or the grim reaper with his sickle at hand, but first would come an idyllic 1980 full of profit and growth.

It seemed to him only right, and certainly Eula wasn't surprised. She had watched her son work intelligently and extremely hard, and now came the payoff the American Dream promised.

Xavier bought a house early in 1980. A modest house — average by Cleveland, Georgia, standards — it wouldn't remain that way for long. It soon became clear that the young, 24-year-old entrepreneur intended to turn the residence into an Alice in Wonderland creation such as the mountain folk had never before seen.

The house grew to *ninety* rooms, with much of the work done by Xavier's brothers. A person could easily get lost in the house, especially on the upper floors where the corridor in places resembles a mysterious maze. A door may lead in four possible directions, only to lead in four more. The house began to resemble a medieval castle, though its appointments might better qualify it as Hugh Hefner's Playboy Mansion Southeast. It had two swimming pools — one indoors, one outdoors. The indoor pool can be entered by careening down a giant slide that stretches from the master bedroom. There were also two jacuzzis, an indoor waterfall, a rooftop greenhouse, a disco, art and photography studios, and a huge garage designed to house the valuable classic cars Xavier had begun to collect.

The first impression one gets of the gigantic house is that it is far too large for one person. The residence of a single Lilliputian, it is designed for Brobdingnagians. It sits atop a hill surrounded by woods, dwarfing the few nearby homes, and is virtually impossible to reach when it rains. The dirt road snaking up to the house, not yet paved, turns into a quagmire when the skies open.

The towering, mammoth house couldn't have been more removed from the reality Xavier had known all of his life. It was almost as if there were no middle ground for him. Being successful in Cleveland, Georgia, on a regional scale, held little appeal for him. He wanted to go from zero to the very top, from a mobile home to a mansion.

Xavier may have inadvertently revealed one of the reasons a mammoth home seemed important to him. "As long as a person knows reality," he said, "fantasy is perfect. The people who get in trouble are those who act like somebody they aren't and start believing it. All my life I've been called kookie. I was the kid with the wild ideas and nobody ever took anything I said seriously. Well, these days if I say somethng like, 'Wouldn't it be fun to charter a Lear jet and fly over to Paris for dinner?' folks assume I might do it."

"Showing" the people who had taunted him about being poor may indeed have been a motive to build a gargantuan domicile and collect exotic automobiles, but surely finances were a reason also. For the first time in his life, Xavier possessed money, a substantial sum of it, and he realized quickly that acquiring finances was the easy part, holding on to them was difficult. The intelligent rich do not put their money in bank savings accounts that pay low interest rates. This is large-

ly the practice of a middle class that will allow their money to
be loaned out at a *higher* interest rate. If anything, Xavier was
shrewd financially — some have called him "tight" — and the
cars and the big house were likely to appreciate in value far
faster than money left in a bank.

The year 1980 would be a good one, Xavier expected, and he
was right. The one nagging problem was finding outlets suffi-
cient to handle the merchandise he wanted to produce, goods
he knew an entire nation would be clamoring for if it had the
awareness of their existence and an easy means by which to
reach them. Price had never been a problem. Often, he had
found, he could have charged more for his babies and
customers would willingly have paid. Nor did he doubt they
would be popular. "Have you run into anyone who hasn't
liked your babies?" he was asked.

"Some have said they don't like them," he answered
sincerely. "But the more they looked at them, the more they
liked them."

The sky did seem to be the limit. In March, 1980, the first
(and Xavier promised they would be the only) set of quintuplets were delivered at Babyland General Hospital, and
adopted to Jeannie and Bennie Shelton of Cumming, Georgia,
for $5,000.

In April, Xavier introduced his "Preemies," miniature Little
People in an edition of five thousand, the result of what was
called a "blackberry winter." The Preemies sold for $100 each
and came with matching birth certificates, adoption papers,
and name tags. More important, they were as popular as
previous editions, enforcing the impression that everything
the young artist turned his hand to became gold. Today these
Preemies are estimated to be worth $450 each.

One of the biggest days in Cleveland's history was April 6,
1980, when Xavier invited the public to participate in his Great
Egg Hunt. More than 5,000 people jammed the tiny town's
streets. Thousands of eggs were hidden on the grounds of
Babyland General Hospital, including fourteen "prize" eggs
and one "golden" egg. The finder of the golden egg was
allowed to adopt the first Preemie.

Rabbits, ducks, and baby chickens were given away, and
there was an Easter Parade featuring people dressed as

storybook characters. It was a festive occasion, children squeal-
ing with delight, cuddly animals everywhere to be squeezed,
Little People stationed about to be ogled by real little people,
and a big triumph for Xavier also. No one in town could doubt
that the "poor Roberts boy" had made something of himself.
Eula watched from the lawn of Dr. Neal's old hospital, her
heart bursting with pride.

On April 7, the day after the Great Egg Hunt, Babyland
General Hospital was closed for a month so it could undergo a
second facelift. The entire building was renovated, and then
all of it was opened to the public on May 8. Bright, eye-
catching murals were painted on the walls; the administrative
part of the business was moved next door to the residence Dr.
Neal had long since called home. The place, from the inside,
really looked like a hospital, but in reality it was one of the
most successful gift shops in America. A big reason for its
popularity was that children, brought along by their parents,
found an ambience not unlike Disney World, or perhaps a
Hollywood movie set. The babies were displayed in utterly
lifelike poses, nursing from a bottle, sitting in a swing,
perhaps cocking a slingshot or riding a hobby horse, and
everywhere were nurses and doctors, weaving fantastic,
delightful tales, much as Xavier had done in the earliest days.

Renovating Babyland General Hospital at this time served a
twofold purpose: not only did it open up a much bigger shopping area and allow the administration offices to move to more
spacious quarters next door, but it shaped the place up for
what was anticipated to be the most important day so far in the
company's history. The highly rated "Real People" television
program was coming to Cleveland on May 9 to get the
lowdown on the Little People.

"This is crazy, even for our show," said "Real People" host
Skip Stephenson, after getting an eyeful of dolls being treated
like real babies, and salespeople insisting politely but firmly
on being addressed as doctors and nurses. It was quite an ad-
mission by Stephenson, as anyone who has seen "Real People"
would understand. The show often features the bizarre and
off-the-wall — people wrestling with bears or sticking their
heads into the mouths of lions, walking across burning coals
with uncovered feet, pulling trucks or train cars with their

teeth, high-diving into six inches of water. Skip Stephenson was not likely to be taken aback, yet what he witnessed was "crazy, even for our show."

The Little People were everywhere on the lawn of Babyland General Hospital, attended by an army of white-clad doctors and nurses. The place resembled a nursery school playground, except it was better tended. Dolls lounged in rocking chairs, hung from swingsets, sat around a picnic basket, cavorted in sandboxes. Some of them held toy baseball bats or clutched miniature footballs. It was a scene that momentarily suspended disbelief this bright, sunshine-filled day, the grass a glorious green, the sky a dazzling blue, the mountain air clean and bracing. But of course it was all make-believe.

"A fascinating story," said "Real People" field producer Tim Hawthorne. "One of the most spectacular I've worked on . . . a fantasy act." Hawthorne couldn't seem to take his eyes off the dolls, who appeared at any moment that they might take on life of their own.

"It's beautiful here," said Marley Klaus, seeing the North Georgia mountains for the first time.

Xavier was nervous. He knew about Skip Stephenson's penchant for clowning, for trivializing, and he'd heard Stephenson use the word "crazy." That's the last thing Xavier wanted to hear. He wanted to listen to phrases such as "delightful fantasy" and "charming make-believe," not something which would poke fun at an entire world he had created and was trying to build upon. It would be easy for Stephenson to take a cheap shot, to portray the operation as a transparent flim-flam with grown people posing as doctors and nurses in order to foist their commercial designs on gullible children. The whole thing could turn into a nightmare if the unpredictable Stephenson adopted this slant.

Stephenson did seem to have the wrong attitude. He was flippant and breezy. He'd asked if there were any female eighteen-year-old Little People with whom he could play. Xavier most definitely did not want his enterprise made the butt of jokes. He had reluctantly agreed to the show because it would be more publicity than Original Appalachian Artworks had ever received, and might launch his babies onto the broad national market he knew they deserved. A person could do a thousand newspaper interviews, appear on a hundred television talk shows, and still not reach the audience of a single showing of "Real People." But if Stephenson made fun of the operation — treated it as a joke — no publicity at all would have to be better than that. It was a gamble. The "Real People" host had promised to "play it straight," but Xavier had numerous haunting doubts.

And they were realized. When the cameras were on, Skip Stephenson started the wisecracks. Xavier searched for a way to reverse what was becoming a disaster, and Skip Stephenson unintentionally gave him the chance. He asked Xavier why the dolls didn't have ears.

"So they can't hear the nasty things you say about them," Xavier retorted. For a moment the two stared at each other. Then both began to laugh. The ice had been broken, and from then on Skip Stephenson allowed himself to become caught up in the fantasy of the Little People.

One scene that day featured the Babyland General Hospital ambulance, siren wailing, lights flashing, screeching to a stop in front of an emergency entrance. A team of attendants frantically wheeled a baby on a stretcher into the hospital. "Everything is going to be all right," said Skip Stephenson to the Little Person. "We've found your blood type: polyester positive."

More filming was done in the next few days at the Spring Valley Country Club in Columbia, South Carolina. This segment had been arranged by The Etc. Shop, an adoption center in Columbia, and it was quite a show. Doctors and nurses arrived from Babyland in a hospital van marked "VERY SPECIAL DELIVERY," while Xavier himself showed up in a 1947 Rolls Royce. All of this was tame compared to other arrivals.

Guests and their Little People made appearances in motorized sailboats, home-made spaceships, race cars, and rolling bubble-filled bathtubs. The parade of Little People parents might have seemed more suited for a circus atmosphere than a network television show, but it was one of the biggest media events in Columbia's history, and local residents went all out. A group of Little People were delivered dangling from the bottom of a helicopter. A sky diver, carrying one of Xavier's dolls, parachuted onto the country club grounds. A spectator called the scene "mass chaos."

Parents and their babies came dressed as lookalikes. Some wore costumes from the Victorian period; others dressed as visitors from outer space. People arrived pulling wagons and pushing buggies. A horse-drawn carriage delivered one family. An incredible 1,200 people, most of them doing something outlandish, showed up at the Spring Valley Country Club in the hope of getting on television. It was a version of Cabbage Patch Madness before the phrase was coined.

Xavier stole the show from Skip Stephenson. The "Real People" host stayed in the background, according to a local newspaper, talking about his upcoming appearance on "The Love Boat" and "nursing his right wrist which had been injured when he slipped and fell while jogging during a break in the filming aboard the boat."

"Meanwhile, Roberts received the majority of the attention as he autographed babies on their soft little bottoms, grinning broadly and speaking to the adoptive parents, asking them questions about the various babies, such as 'Has Bobby Rae been a good little boy?' "

The "Real People" crew seemed astounded by the remarks of the people who had adopted a Little Person. What they heard was the advance guard of the craze that would reach full flowering in 1983. "I love my babies!" one woman shouted. "I wouldn't go anywhere without them!"

"My friends all laughed at me when I got my first one," another woman said. "But guess what? All my friends have babies now."

"Oh yes," said a third woman. "I change her Pampers every day. She's lovable and she's quiet."

This sort of reaction might have been manufactured in Cleveland, Georgia, but no matter what else one might have thought of it, it was clearly genuine and unrehearsed in Columbia, South Carolina. The producers of "Real People" didn't know it at the time, but they were getting a preview of what later would become a countrywide phenomenon.

Xavier brought Otis Lee with him (the two are almost inseparable in public appearances), and the Little People's ringleader danced with a nurse to a jazz band rendition of "Baby Face." The idea caught on. Soon the floor was packed with adults dancing, each one with a Little Person as a partner. The "Real People" cameras caught it all.

The show aired on November 19, 1980, and is credited as being a landmark in the history of the Cabbage Patch Kids. Skip Stephenson made a mistake during the show, saying the dolls "sold for one thousand dollars each." The next day the switchboard at Babyland General Hospital was jammed with calls from individuals who wanted to adopt the "Thousand Dollar Baby." Except for the quintuplets, of course, no doll that Xavier had manufactured had sold for that much.

But if nothing else, Xavier was an opportunist. The idea for the Grand Edition had been born. One thousand dolls, selling for $1,000 each, were soon available for adoption. These were standing babies, each one signed by Xavier, and again Xavier learned he had not miscalculated by charging too much. At this point, the question had to be asked, Was any price too high? One thousand dolls at $1,000 each was a cool $1,000,000 in merchandise!

The appearance on "Real People" also inspired the issuance of the Celebrity Edition, five thousand dolls priced at $200 each. The dolls were dressed in red and white "I'm a Little TV Celebrity" T-shirts, each signed by Xavier, and Linda Allen was listed as the "mother" of the edition in honor of her rôle in bringing "Real People" and the Little People together. Celebrity Edition babies are now estimated to be worth $400.

"Real People" was just the start of nationwide publicity in 1980 that no amount of money could have bought. An advertisement is an advertisement, no matter how clever and arresting it might be. A news story or an appearance on a television show, on the other hand, carries with it the suggestion that something worthwhile and noteworthy is taking place. *Time* magazine, September 8, 1980, in a story titled "Bundles of Polyester Joy," was one of the first national publications to sense something big was going on in north Georgia.

The little darlings are parentless and begging to be taken home. They do not come from stork, or test tube, but from a former medical clinic in Cleveland, Ga. called Babyland

General. They are dolls. Each fabric-and-polyester infant is a "soft sculpture," handmade by one of 125 employees of Entrepreneur Xavier Roberts, 24, a former artist. In just two years, Babyland has "delivered" 50,000 babies at prices of $125 to $200 each, which Roberts insists on calling adoption fees. "You don't buy them, you adopt them," said one middle-aged Miami woman, pressing a fat baby boy to her ample bosom. Too enhance the illusion, all Babyland employees are required to dress as hospital staff; Roberts is the white-coated "doctor." Customers — or rather, prospective parents — must raise their right hands and take an oath to love and care for their little charges. At the Georgia plant and a branch "adoption center" in Orlando, Fla., Roberts plans eventually to produce adult dolls as well. Each will come equipped with a driver's license and birth certificate — everything but credit cards and the right to vote.

Coleco has taken a great number of bows for the marketing job it did in making the Cabbage Patch Kids the hottest Christmas item of the 1983 or any other season, and many of the kudos were deserved. Yet much of the Coleco strategy had already been used by Xavier, who by himself had proved he could generate massive, favorable publicity. What Xavier lacked was not the ability to promote himself or his product, but the far-reaching distribution channels at Coleco's command. Without the outlets where people could adopt the babies, Xavier could never hope to achieve full potential for his merchandise.

Through all of the 1980 fanfare, Xavier exhibited no signs of getting a big head. Outwardly he was the same, a quiet, rather shy (except when spinning tales about his babies), unpretentious soul. Designer fashions — one of his ads would read "Calvin Who?" — were on his agenda, but he was hardly a fancy dresser himself. Blue jeans, T-shirts, and tennis shoes were more normal attire than tuxedos. The giant house he was renovating, and the expensive cars, were two of his very few ostentatious displays of wealth. And it was unlikely anyone could have found the house without directions. It was set on an out-of-the-way country road that carried little traffic.

Nor were Xavier's leisure-time activities, such as they were, the kind likely to make a jet-setter blush with envy. Occasionally he would drink with friends, or visit old school chums at a local pizza parlor, but there was nothing expensive about his tastes. There was no question, however, of his status as a V.I.P. in Cleveland. He was the town's largest employer, the main source of jobs. When the Talon zipper factory laid off a number of workers, Xavier was able to take them aboard Original Appalachian Artworks. It was sweet revenge, if this were what he sought, against those who had made fun of him as a child because he was poor.

Life for Xavier was still mostly work. There were dozens of natural offshoots the doll business lent itself to — clothes, other accessories for the dolls, books, magazines, fan clubs, TV, movies, etc. — and Xavier explored them all. Walt Disney, an individual whose life he tried to emulate, had not been content to draw Mickey Mouse and Donald Duck comic strips. The potential was just as great with the Cabbage Patch Kids. One area of enterprise that interested Xavier immediately was a gigantic amusement park, another Disney World but with Little People characters and themes, where parents and their children could visit to immerse themselves in fantasy.

Trade shows were still important, and even more important was the burgeoning adoption center business. These eventually would grow to number more than two thousand in the United States alone, with additional centers overseas. Yet these were mainly small businesses with limited sales potential. The Little People, Xavier remained convinced, needed to be in the largest mass-market department stores.

Everything pointed to Xavier being right. *Paris Match*, the most widely read magazine in France, said the Little People "have forever left the category of mere toys to become real babies."

Meanwhile, the fantasy continued to be built upon. Original Appalachian Artworks printed "The Legend of the Cabbage Patch Kids": Many Years Ago A Young Boy Named Xavier Roberts Happened Upon An Enchanted Cabbage Patch Where He Found Very Special Little People Who Call Themselves Cabbage Patch Kids. To Help Fulfill The Cabbage Patch Kids' Dream Of Having Families With Whom To Share Their Love,

Xavier Set Out In Search Of Parents To Adopt Them — A Search That Will Continue As Long As There Are Children Looking For Love.

Whatever one thinks of the "Cabbage Patch Legend," the fantasy sold. And it sold not just because people thought the dolls might be good buys. Evidence mounted incontrovertibly that many "parents" became genuinely attached to their babies. Some said they wouldn't sell at any price, it would be like bartering away a son or daughter. The fact is that in the past other people have seemed to feel the same way about different dolls, and usually these are never for resale until the owner has passed away.

The Grand Edition dolls prompted by Skip Stephenson's mistake were something to see. They were dressed in evening gowns, mink coats, and the males in elegant tuxedos. The females wore diamond earrings, the males diamond cuff links. The birth certificates were printed in "money green," and each doll came with $1,000 in Otis Lee Reserve Notes "redeemable in fun." Of course, both males and females were impeccably groomed, and were guaranteed by Xavier "to become the most popular and socially acceptable Little People ever."

The Grand Edition dolls were aimed exclusively at upper-middle-class and wealthy people and collectors. The snob appeal — "socially acceptable" — was inherent in the promotion. Interestingly, the Grand Edition babies, while retaining their value, were the first put out by Xavier that have not yet increased in value.

While Xavier was committed to finding a much broader market for his merchandise, he wasn't willing to take the first opportunity that came along. He was firmly persuaded of the rightness of his own sales concepts, and could be extremely stubborn in insisting they be followed to the letter. "I was convinced," he says, "that my Kids should be made and marketed by a quality oriented company with a long-term commitment to the concept of Cabbage Patch Kids.They had to understand the adoption concept, the look and feeling of the doll."

(This was not just talk. The first package Coleco designed to hold the doll was flatly rejected by Xavier, who had retained control over the matter. "It was just plain unattractive, what they wanted to do," he says. "What finally came about was much more aesthetically pleasing.")

The insistence on doing it "his way" would prove an important factor in Xavier's ultimate success. In spite of his desire for riches, or more accurately because of it, he would not proceed with a project unless he was thoroughly satisfied with the method in which it was being handled. Adoption was an example. No matter that the dolls could be sold more quickly if the rigamarole of the adoption was let pass; prospective parents had to take the oath. A short-term gain, Xavier felt, could be a long-term loss. Similarly with the way the dolls were displayed. He didn't want them in a setting where they looked like dolls. They should be doing what a baby would be doing, playing with a toy, holding a bottle of milk, peering through the bars of a playpen. If the buyer didn't want to display them as Xavier thought, the buyer could find another product to sell. Too many businesses, Xavier felt instinctively, had let little things slip, procedures which had made them successful to begin with, and the results were always eventually negative.

About this time a man who would become very important in Xavier's life was getting his first look at a Little Person. This was Roger Schlaifer, who grew up in Silver Spring, Maryland, but now owned an advertising agency in Atlanta. "One day,"Schlaifer recalls, "I was shocked to see the really ugly doll my wife, Susanne, brought home. She said it was art, an investment. But she couldn't get it away from our six-year old daughter, Jessica Barrett. We didn't put the doll on the shelf. Jessica and our other daughter, Veronica Ellis, still interact with the doll."

Roger Schlaifer studied the doll his daughters had become so attached to, watched as they took it to school for a show-and-tell, wondered as they treated it almost like another human being, and slowly he began to think there might be something special here. He contacted Xavier and tried to get the advertising account.

"They weren't interested," Schlaifer says. "They were doing fine on their own. They were growing spectacularly. Roberts had copyrighted everything about the doll, though there are a good many housewives knocking them off in their kitchen."

Indeed, the last thing Xavier needed was an advertising program. The Little People were getting free publicity in large, unremitting doses. There weren't enough hours in the day to talk with everyone who wanted an interview. And it was good advertising, because the stories were almost invariably favorable. Xavier made good impressions on reporters who talked with him. They were accustomed to fast-talking hustlers with glad hands and plastic smiles, and found instead a young mountain man who was modest, shy, sincere, and down-to-earth. They waited for him to lapse into cynicism when he rambled on about his "babies," but it didn't happen. The logical resort was to write or say something favorable.

Schlaifer had not landed an advertising account, but he found himself in agreement with Xavier that the Little People deserved a big future. And the more he thought about the matter, the more he wanted to be part of it. He developed a licensing plan for the Little People, based on Xavier's cabbage patch story, and presented it to the young artist. It was exactly what Xavier had in mind. The advertising agency, Schlaifer Nance and Company, became the exclusive licensing agent for the Cabbage Patch Kids. The relationship of ad company and artist would prove profitable for everyone. It would turn out to be a bonanza.

Schlaifer Nance & Company ultimately made the deal that brought Coleco into the picture. In addition, as the *Washington Post* pointed out, "Some 50 other companies are making Cabbage Patch products: baby and children's clothes, bedding, throw rugs, color forms, cosmetics, the biggest selling sticker book in history, lunch boxes and thermos bottles, Parker Bros. board and card games, riding toys, and books and records, among others."

The big plans Roger Schlaifer outlined had dovetailed with Xavier's own conception of how big the product could be. "Cabbage Patch Kids," says Schlaifer, "unlike most other licensed products, is not limited to one or two characters for merchandising possibilities. Instead, like the Kids, with their multiple looks, names and personalities, there is a variety which gives manufacturers unlimited creative range to develop interesting and unique products. Cabbage Patch Kids aren't tied to any one color scheme, for example, so customers don't get bored with the presentation. And a very important concept is the spirit or whimsy that is a part of each and every product."

Chain Store Age, practically begging to be corrected, asked Xavier, "Why did you decide to bring the dolls to the mass market?"

"You mean Kids," Xavier replied. "I knew from the reaction of the people who adopted my babies that they would have mass appeal. The idea of the adoption plus the care and concern that parents feel towards their Kids is genuine. But the prices were out of line for the mass market, so we needed to find a way to get the Kids into a broader market."

And again Roger Schlaifer, on what he's done and what he intends to do: "Cabbage Patch Kids is more than a character; it's a total concept, an umbrella, tying it to a myriad of products and therefore giving it brand appeal; and, perhaps more importantly, we have long-term commitments from our manufacturers for quality, growth and competitive pricing. Every company has committed substantial dollars to making sure the concept develops year by year. We are married to long-term goals and growth."

But towards the end of 1980, this all remained in the future. What occupied Xavier's thoughts at this time were plans for his coming Christmas Extravaganza, which he intended to be the largest single event in Cleveland's history. The date of the Extravaganza was December 14, and the party exceeded even Xavier's rather grandiose expectations.

Fifteen thousand people, almost ten times the population of the town, showed up. The streets of Cleveland were jammed. Thousands of lights had been strung on buildings and trees, and even automobiles were decorated in the holiday spirit. Music filled the air, and there were cheers when Santa Claus, followed by his elves, arrived to talk with the throngs of children.

Hanging from the chimney of the administration building was what was advertised as the World's Largest Christmas Stocking, and indeed it might have been. It measured 36 feet in length, 240 inches in circumference, and it was bursting with gifts. Santa Claus supervised the lighting of the gigantic Christmas tree.

Xavier made a grand entrance, decked out in a tuxedo and flanked by bodyguards, stepping out of his Rolls Royce limousine to cheering more hearty and enthusiastic than even Santa Claus had received. It was a proud moment for the young artist, barely turned twenty-five — a triumphant moment. He headed for the porch of the administration building, a hero in his own town, where he happily signed autographs for what seemed an endless queue of admirers.

Otis Lee arrived in a second limousine. The future presidential candidate was accompanied by his nanny and the Staff Stork.

Xavier had spared no expense. Hundreds of prizes were given away; there always seemed to be a new drawing taking place, including twenty-eight Little People and two Grand Edition babies. A ton of "snow" was flown in from Paramount Studios to lend realism to the winter scene. As darkness fell there was a gigantic fireworks show, by far the most spectacular ever witnessed in north Georgia, the lights flaring, bursting, exploding, bright lights of all colors, beautiful in the clear night sky.

Xavier himself was the brightest light of all on this crisp, nippy December day. He sat on the porch of the administration building for hours (the impression was he would stay forever), welcoming child after child, and plenty of adults also, signing his name over and over, spinning tales, smiling shyly, his eyes shining like the Christmas Star. It would be something to remember on the long cold winter nights of his own future.

Many of those who stood in line this December 14 were employees of Xavier. There were now a staggering (for Cleveland) three hundred and fifty of these. Many were his friends and neighbors, but things would never be the same between them. There was respect in their eyes and even admiration; but one could also sense a degree of fear. Fear that only money, and the sheer power of it, can instill.

Xavier could have been standing atop one of the nearby mountains, so high did he feel, exhilarated, filled with what he had done. By every conceivable method of thinking, it was his day.

7

Dolls in History

The profession Xavier decided to pursue — doll-making — is hardly what pops to mind when today's "careers of the future" are discussed. The modern rage is high-tech. That's what Horace Greeley, were he living today, might advise a young man to head toward. The U.S. is in the midst of a great technological revolution, featuring the silicon chip, information processing, satellite communications, all the glittering miracles of the Space Age. We look to the stars, not the buried ruins of antiquity. Come up with something new, perhaps the old adage should be rewritten, and the world will beat a path to your doorstep.

What Xavier chose was something old. The human race, for 25,000 years, according to anthropologists, almost for its entire history, has been modeling its own figure in effigy. This gives the doll, according to Janet Johl, author of the classic *The Fascinating Story of Dolls*, "the right to be classified as one of the first inventions of the human race."

The first dolls were cult objects used both to control nature and to house the spirits that early man worshipped. The dolls were credited with having life, and later with possessing divine life. "Thus," writes Janet Johl, "the inspiration of the artist of antiquity was never a dead thing but on the contrary was very alive."

Dolls in Egypt, dedicated to Osiris, have been discovered in ancient Egyptian sarcophagi, buried with little girls. Some Egyptian dolls were called *Ushabti*, and peasants believed that after they died they would go to an afterworld where the

Ushabti did all the work. A pleasant thought, no doubt, for history records that these people performed backbreaking labor. Nevertheless, Xavier might consider the research of Janet Johl. "The demand for these magical mummy-servants was so great that they were actually produced by a factory method in the later dynasties and the result was a deterioration in workmanship, and Ushabti figures that grew smaller and smaller."

The British Museum in London contains Egyptian dolls dating back to the Middle Kingdom, centuries before the birth of Christ, taken from the tombs of children and considered of inestimable value. Ancient Egyptian dolls can also be seen in the United States, at the University of Pennsylvania Museum and at the Metropolitan Museum of Art in New York City.

Numerous dolls were uncovered at the purported site of Troy. Ancient Greek girls often dedicated their dolls to Aphrodite and Artemis, and boys to Hermes and Apollo. The sixth book of the *Anthologia Palatine* contains the following epigram: "Timareta, the daughter of Timaretus, before her wedding, hath dedicated to thee, Artemis of the lake, her tambourine and her pretty ball and the caul that kept up her hair, and her dolls, too, and their dresses; a virgin's gift as is fit, to a virgin Diana. But, daughter of Leto, hold thy hand over the girl, and purely keep her in purity."

Interestingly, the identical word in Greek is used for "girl" and "doll."

Roman children played with dolls, and they have been found in the catacombs beneath the Vatican, indicating they had been playthings for the offspring of Christian martyrs. In the Saturnalia in Rome, a special feature was presenting dolls to children, and the dolls often were dedicated to Venus, Goddess of Love. Miniature furniture was constructed upon which the dolls could sit and lie down.

Anthropologists believe there is probably not a country on earth where dolls have not been made, nor has it been possible to trace mankind back far enough to a time when there were no dolls. They have been discovered from the Macedonian epoch, 25,000 years ago. The incredible, awe-provoking stories the dolls tell, and also ones they hide, are nothing less than the history of humanity.

Inside an ancient Tibetan doll, accidentally broken open in New York, was found a stunningly beautiful ruby, and a stick, running from the base of the head, to which had been attached twelve rolls of parchment written on in an unknown script. The bottom of the stick was honed razor sharp, and was used to prick rodents that would drop dead from the poisoning.

John H. Shaw, writing for the *Club Bulletin* of the National Doll and Toy Collectors Club, Inc., described the culture of an African tribe by saying, "A Masai has but two occupations, one is hunting and the other is carving out these dolls. Their work, if done by civilized people, would be considered good. Done by the supposedly ignorant natives, they are little short of marvelous. A Masai does his carving as he does everything, with skill and thoroughness. Many of their dolls have the actual articles of dress on them; neckbands, the decorative fur loin cloth, the fur leg band, spears, skin shields and other details all in miniature."

In ancient India, children were thrown into the sacred Ganges to appease the goddess who presided over the river's destiny. Later, a more enlightened ruler substituted dolls for the children. And in the north of Argentina exists a people who make dolls only when someone dies, and the doll is a replica of the deceased.

Just as dolls were substituted for living children in India, so too did they spare many lives in other parts of the world. The following horrifying account comes from Japan, possibly from the year 3 A.D.:

Tenth month, fifth day: Yamato-hiko, the Mikado's younger brother by his mother's side, died.

Eleventh month, second: Yamato-hiko was buried at Tsukizaka in Musa. Thereupon his personal attendants were assembled, and were all buried alive upright in the precinct of the tomb. For several days they died not, but wept and wailed day and night. As last they died and rotted. Dogs and crows gathered and ate them.

This barbaric practice, which had existed for centuries, was mercifully halted by the Emperor shortly after the mass burial, though some have questioned the righteousness of his motivation. It was felt he believed dead servants were good for nobody, while live ones could continue to serve the privileged aristocracy. An entire way of life was being threatened. The best and brightest functionaries systematically were being wiped out. To remedy the situation, yet not admit to his subjects the bankruptcy of his own policy, the Emperor ruled that dolls could replace humans in the mass graves.

The same indefensible slaughter took place in Egypt. The head man, ever superstitious, wanted to make sure he would go into the afterlife with the same faithful cortege which had served him on earth. And the practice probably was ended for the same reason in Japan, with the same solution: the substitution of dolls. Clara Hallard Fawcett, in her book *Dolls: A New Guide for Collectors*, writes, "In a Pharaoh's tomb many other things accompanied the image of wives, sweethearts and retainers — small fishing ships with their crews, pleasure boats, workshops, cattle, shepherds, etc."

The Etruscans, who dominated central Italy from the eighth to the fourth century B.C., traditionally placed dolls and other precious objects belonging to deceased leaders inside their coffins in the belief they would be useful in an afterlife. The rationalization was that the dolls would come to life and replace the images in whom they'd been made, thus assuring a continued comfortable existence. Of course, no similar provisions were deemed necessary for less exalted members of society.

In Mongolia dolls finally replaced an even more hideous practice. When a chieftain died, the most attractive children in his family were forced to swallow quicksilver until they died ... so their "freshness" of color would please the chieftain.

Some of the most fascinating early dolls are from China. The "tilting doll," for example, was so perfectly balanced it couldn't be knocked over. No matter how you struck the doll, it always returned to its original position, a design specifically intended to enforce the idea that Buddha could never fall. A Japanese doll, *Oki-Agari-Koboshi*, was made to perform the same function. It was modeled in the image of Bodhidharma, the Buddhist priest who in 520 A.D. sailed from India to China and founded a sect which the Japanese know as Zen. This doll is always sitting and has no feet because Bodhidharma spent nine years on a rock without moving.

The Chinese also produced the "doctor doll," which served a practical purpose. Chinese women would not permit doctors to examine them, but by using the doctor doll they could point to the area of the body where they were experiencing pain. A relative of the doctor doll was used to teach students to insert their acupuncture needles.

The origin of the word "doll" is not known, though it likely can be traced to the Greek *eidolen,* meaning idol. Nor is it known whether playing with dolls by children is instinctive. Some experts do not think so. The young in primitive tribes need to be taught what to do with a doll, as do certain isolated mountain children in the Carolinas.

Even recently in the United States, though far more common in Europe during the Middle Ages, supernatural powers of healing have been attributed to certain dolls, with sick children being brought to them in pilgrimages in the hope that touching the doll would effect a cure.

Dolls are perhaps more accurate history teachers than historians. Archeologist Mary F. Curtis, writing about dolls excavated in Northern Greece, said, "The inspiration which has animated this clay emanated from a center of the most refined invention, and skillful fingers fashioned it by precepts of traditional culture. The works in question give us the actual costume of their period with fidelity, and, in the features and gestures of their personages, they transcribe countless shades and phases of thoroughly human sentiment. These sympathetic and natural charms are not confined to any place or time, and consequently an element of undying youth and freshness has been secured. The physical resemblances, like the make of the garments, are not closely localized. They have been disseminated equally in all quarters of the globe. Hence the astonishingly modern aspect of these models and relics of the past."

Dolls have been popular with an immense number of very famous historical personages, just a few of whom include Madame DuBarry, Madame La Pompadour, Louis Napoleon, King Charles IV, Louis XVI, Queen Isabella, Marie Antoinette, Queen Victoria, the Emperor Maximilian, Empress Alexandra of Russia, William Penn, William Pitt, Benjamin Franklin, and George Washington. Many of these had dolls modeled after them, and the dolls usually were eagerly sought after and prized.

Dolls played an important role in the history of Christianity. Perhaps the first known references to them were the sermons of St. John Chrysostom (circa 400 A.D.), who mentioned the existence of a holy crib occupied by figures of the Holy Family. In the Middle Ages, churches, convents, and monasteries were filled with miniature doll representations of the Nativity scene, as were many homes. Whether called the Spanish *nacimientos*, Mexican *Posados*, Italian *precipio*, French *crèche*, or German *krippe*, the doll figures represented Jesus, Mary, Joseph, the three kings, shepherds, angels, and farm animals. The finest artists of the day arranged depictions of the Nativity, and much of what they produced was art of the first order.

The Catholic Church owned almost all of the original crèche dolls, some of which became virtually priceless, others made valuable by accessories. At the Franciscan Church in Rome, for instance, is the Jeweled Bambino, a crude model of Jesus which wears a crown of jewels, silk garments, and has feet of gold. Early Catholics donated dolls to the church as atonement for their sins.

But quality gradually declined as more and more people wanted the dolls. As with the *Ushabti*, the terrific demand led to a production speedup and the subsequent lessening of fine craftsmanship.

The earliest toy dolls (as opposed to dolls to ward off spirits, appease spirits, house dead people to keep them from bothering the living, etc.) came from Greece and Egypt. The first toy proper was probably a rattle-box, used in Africa, still in vogue in the U.S. today. An article that appeared in the magazine *St. Nicholas*, November, 1879, written by Olive Thorne, is perhaps the definitive statement on the early history of dolls and toys.

> The second toy was, doubtless, a doll, for that fascinating object has been in use from the earliest times of which we have any record, by all peoples, barbarous or civilized. The English name is said by some of the wise men to be a nickname for Dorothea, while others think it a contraction

of "idol." When we see the affection of little people for their dolls, this origin seems probable. The French call a doll a *poupée* and the Germans *puppe*. The pronunciation differs in the two languages, but both names come from the Latin *pupa*, a girl. Before the 18th century, dolls were called "little ladies" or "babies."

The dignified science of history is too much taken up with stories of the wars and troubles of grown-up people to tell us what the little ancients used to play with; but we have found out many things in spite of the big books. Out of the ground are being dug, nowadays, ruined cities and treasures of the people of long ago, among them the precious toys of children. Thus we have found out that the little people of the island of Cyprus, in the Mediterranean, who lived three thousand years ago, had toys of terra cotta, figures of animals, of horses on platforms which ran on four terra cotta wheels, with riders of curious form, some on their knees, and others holding in each arm a large jar; donkeys with panniers, two-wheeled vehicles like our drays, and chariots with horses and drivers. Then they had a representation of some game — whether of child or man — several figures with joined hands, dancing around one standing still . . .

The ancient little Egyptians, three or four thousand years ago, had dolls, painted to represent clothes, with arms and legs moving on pins by means of strings, so that if they couldn't take off their clothes, they could move about. Some were very crude, without limbs, and for hair they had thick and long strings of beads. They also had figures washing, or kneading bread, which could be worked by pulling strings, and crocodiles which would open their mouths by the same means . . .

The first toy of the ancient Greek baby was a rattle-box; then came — as he grew — dolls of clay (a sort of coarse china doll), figures of animals, apes with their little ones, ducks, tortoises, and others.

The first doll to be brought to what is now the United States was given in 1607 to a Virginia Indian girl by a member of Sir

Walter Raleigh's expedition, commanded by Captain John Smith. The event was captured beautifully by the expedition's artist, John White, and a copy of his painting is displayed at the Smithsonian Institution in Washington, D.C. Wrote a member of the historic expedition: "They are greatlye Dilighted with pupetts and babes which wear broughte oute of England." Judging from the little girl's joyous expression in John White's painting, the writer did not exaggerate.

The oldest *existing* doll to be carried to the United States is said to be "Letitia Penn," a Queen Anne, twenty inches high, made of velvet and striped brocade, wearing a full court dress stretched by crinoline. Letitia Penn was brought from England by William Penn as a gift for a friend of his daughter, and now, because of its age and rarity, commands considerable value.

Obviously, there were many dolls in America long before the colonists came. The Hopi Indians whittled their magnificent Katchina dolls, and the Navajos also made splendid dolls, in addition to their beautiful blankets. In any tribe — the Taos Indians, Pueblo, Apache, Seminole, Creek, Kiowa, Blackhawk, Chippewa, Cherokee, Chickasaw, Zuni, Arapaho, Shoshone, Sioux, Comanche, Crow, Cheyenne, Seneca, Oneida, Blackfoot, Plains, Iroquois — there are exquisitely crafted dolls, bright and colorful creations, dolls which relate the customs and history of a proud, talented and largely peaceful people.

Xavier Roberts has come under considerable criticism for calling his dolls "babies," yet less than two hundred years ago it was they who now criticize who would have been out of step. In America, up to that time, *all* dolls were called babies, even though many of them were in the form of grown women.

The elegant dolls brought from Europe for the enjoyment of wealthy colonists, dolls often decked out in finery modeled after that worn in the English court, were not really typical of what are known as colonial dolls. These were usually homemade, whittled from maple or pine, and of course were without the latest continental fashions.

The first doll patent (#19,770, March 30, 1858) issued in the United States was granted to Ludwig Greiner, listed in the Philadelphia Directory as a "Toy Man," address "441 Coates

St., Philadelphia." Many collectors believe they have an original Greiner, and those who do possess an object of significant worth.

Ludwig Greiner was born in Germany, birthplace of many of the master dollmakers, and although his creations have been called the "all-American doll," the styles actually were copied from German models. A Greiner doll, said a prominent collector, "reminds one of an old aunt who has a cupboard full of cold fried chicken, and cream cookies, they are so gentle and placid ... but many of them have shoulders like Jack Dempsey."

"The Greiners do look well bred," wrote Janet Johl, "well fed, sweet and placid. Some of them are almost beautiful, in the way that age brings forth a mellow beauty, not the beauty of the sculptor or the artist. They usually have high foreheads,and small noses and small mouths. Their eyes, which are either 'set in,' or painted, are wide open, and the hair, drawn back, almost invariably shows the lobes of the ears. These indestructible heads were sold separately, and industrious mothers usually made the bodies at home. These dolls never broke. They were sturdy and durable, made for hard play and not for ornamental use. They just wore out, and so they are often found in bad condition with scarred noses, home-made worn and torn shoes, and bodies misshapen. Sometimes the hands and feet are of carved wood. More often they are of cloth and leather."

Another famous American doll was manufactured by Albert Schoenhut, who came from a long line of toy-making families in Germany. He invented the "Schoenhut Toy Piano" which was popular for decades, but he is most remembered for his dolls. "The principal feature of the Doll," said his son George Schoenhut, "was the unbreakable nature of the parts and the indestructible metal joints. The joints were so mounted that the springs in them would compress if they were pulled rather than stretched. This made the life of the doll almost endless."

Who else but Thomas Edison would have invented the mechanism for the talking doll. A small phonograph with discs fit into the doll's body, and by changing the discs, the doll was able to "say" different things. The Edison dolls operated when a key was turned which wound a spring which in turn activated the phonograph.

A doll replaced a baby in the 1925 motion picture "New Toys." It was called the Bye-Lo Baby, and was so realistic on film that it was impossible to tell the difference between the doll and a genuine infant. The Bye-Lo Baby became one of the most popular dolls ever produced; it wore cap, dress, diaper, booties, and thanks to Thomas Edison, it could cry.

Even more popular and long-lasting was the teddy bear, named for President Theodore Roosevelt, who on a 1902 bear hunting trip to Mississippi refused to shoot a bear cub he suddenly came across. The incident, especially the thought of the cute, cuddly, and vulnerable cub, inspired a small store owner in Brooklyn, Morris Michtom, to make the first teddy bear. He wrote to Roosevelt at the White House, asking permission to use the President's name, and surprisingly, the hero of San Juan Hill responded, saying he didn't know what his name was worth, but Michtom was welcome to use it if he wanted.

The teddy bear was a hit from the start. It was a fad which turned into a craze, similar to the Cabbage Patch Kids, though devoid of the sacking of stores and violence. Everyone wanted a teddy bear, and production couldn't keep pace with demand, even though more than a dozen firms, foreign and domestic, had pirated the idea and were manufacturing their own versions.

Just as the *Wall Street Journal* viewed the Cabbage Patch Craze as a dark omen, so was the teddy bear regarded with misgivings in the early 1900s. A priest in Michigan said it was destroying all instincts of motherhood and leading to race suicide! A magazine editor, while not as pessimistic as the Michigan priest, nonetheless saw no good coming out of the teddy bear mania. "It is enough to make a perfect lady of a doll mad. The dear little girls who have always cried for dolls at Christmas are this year crying for Teddy Bears, and dolls are left on shelves to cry the paint off their pretty cheeks because of the neglect. So great is the demand for Teddy Bears, which range in price from ninety-eight cents to $12.00, that the factories can't keep up the supply, and what makes it still more alarming is that factories are supplying sweaters, overalls, jackets, and so forth for the bears. Will it be as pretty a sight when a little girl mothers a bear as when she mothered a doll?"

Sages were predicting a short life for the teddy bear. "Bears will drop out of sight after the first of the year," predicted a prominent retailer. "Bears on their last legs," he said the next year. Sears Roebuck, more astutely, decided at the same time that "Teddy has come to stay."

Teddy bears were dressed as baseball players, with the stands packed with other teddy bears, as boxers, and as football players. The Circus at Madison Square Garden dressed its clowns and trick dogs as teddy bears. Vaudevillians told bad jokes. "If Theodore Roosevelt is President of the United States with his clothes on, what is he with his clothes off?

"Teddy Bare!"

One of the original teddy bears is on display at Sagamore Hill, Theodore Roosevelt's home, a gift from Morris Michtom's son. And the teddy bear still sells, almost eighty years after the prediction of its imminent demise, a staple of American life. Like Mom and apple pie.

Dolls played a role in both world wars, particularly the first. In 1913 Germany had a virtual monopoly on doll production, manufacturing more than two-thirds of all the dolls made in the world. That same year German shoppers were urged to buy blonde dolls, not brunette, so their children would learn the worth of "inborn racial unity." It seems that Kaiser Wilhelm, and Adolf Hitler after him, shared common beliefs.

The war began in 1914, and doll exports (doll manufacturing was considered a "key" industry) were cut off overnight. In most of the world it was impossible to acquire spare doll parts. The result was that many countries — including the U.S., Japan, England, France — entered the doll world, stealing copyrights with impunity. In France it was called "The Renaissance of the French Doll," the U.S. exported "Unbreakable dolls," while England produced "art dolls." The Japanese imitations of German dolls were superior to those emanating from America, which were considered "much coarser."

The dolls produced during World War I in France were quite beautiful. Prior to the war, the French simply had not been able to compete with the Germans. French doll factories were located near cities, where the cost of living was high, while Germany employed peasant labor in manufacturing concerns set in the remote countryside. (The comparison to the Cabbage Patch Kids is interesting. Coleco set up its manufacturing outlets in the Far East, not in the foothills of the Appalachians, where the cost of labor is low for America, but exceptionally high compared to Asia.)

French dolls, fitted out by the finest Parisian dressmakers, were sent along with other art treasures on a ship which traveled all over the world. The purpose was propaganda, and it was engaged in by all countries. The English put a high priority on the manufacture of a doll which resembled a British soldier, and a series depicting the Royal Family.

Dolls were used to raise money. Madame Paderewski, wife of the famous pianist, sponsored dolls for Polish relief. They were named Jan and Halka, the "Waifs of Cracow," and were manufactured in large quantities. "Health and Happiness to you, kind doll lover," read the medal which came with the Waifs, "who by taking into your heart and home one of my little doll waifs of Poland, have fed a starving mother or child in that 'saddest land' — Helena Paderewski."

Parachute dolls were supposed to be dropped over southern U.S. cities in 1941, each with a capsule attached to its leg and a message contained in the capsule. The idea was the brainchild of the British American Ambulance Corps, and money was offered to the first delivering the message to the mayor of his city. During World War II, crudely made Hitler and Mussolini and Tojo dolls were manufactured so children and adults alike could throw baseballs, rocks, and darts at them.

Great music has been composed for dolls: *Marionette Operas* (Haydn); *The Doll's Cradle Song* (Bizet); *Petrouchka Suite* (Stravinsky); *The Golliwog Cake Walk* (Debussy); *Doll Song*, from *Tales of Hoffman* (Offenbach); *March of the Tin Soldier* (Tchaikovsky); and *March of the Toys* (Victor Herbert).

A major selling point for dolls in this period was that "you can't break them," the boast of many dollmakers, but it often crumbled like their creations in the hands of children. However, dollmaker Sol D. Hoffman really did have a tough product, and connoisseurs of violence would have enjoyed watching his salesmen at work. The salesmen would pound the dolls' heads on the floor, as a would-be buyer watched, toss them against walls, bang on them with hammers, drive nails into their skulls, a seeming madman bent on destruction. Hoffman was a dollmaker who lasted.

One of the most popular dolls of all time is the Raggedy Ann (and Raggedy Andy), which first appeared on the market in 1919, modeled after the main character in a series of children's books written by Johnny Gruelle. A good-condition early Raggedy Ann is a collectible of substantial worth.

There have been numerous dolls on the American scene, the following being merely a tip-of-the-iceberg sample: Deb-U Dolls; Flossie Flirt (this one flirted with you by rolling its eyes); Dutch Dolls; Creeping Dolls (dolls that literally crept along); Scarlett O'Hara Doll; Blessed Event Doll; Sunny Jim Doll; Vogue Dolls; Saralee Dolls; Mr. T. Doll; New-Born Babe; Patsy Dolls (the Pat-a-Pat, which cried and clapped its hands, was a big seller); Peddler Dolls (modeled after street vendors); Charles Lindbergh Doll; Charlie McCarthy Doll; Mortimer Snerd Doll; Prince Charming Doll; Jackie Coogan Doll; Pinnochio Doll; Blue Fairy Doll; Seven Dwarfs Dolls; Shirley Temple (another which was super-popular); Baby Bumps Doll; Campbell Kid (put out in conjunction with the soup company); Toni Doll (had washable hair made of nylon — the Dupont Company was so proud of the doll that it paid for the advertising); Webber Singing Doll (it sang); Baby Coos (it cooed); Patti Prays (it prayed); Betsy Wetsy (it wet); Billiken (supposed to bring good luck); Beating Heart Doll (its heart beat); Gibson Girl; Frozen Charlotte Dolls; Patty Comfort; Little Genius Dolls; Dick Tracy Dolls; Sparkle Plenty Dolls; Joe Palooka Dolls; Ducky; Tickletoes; Algy (a doll with no allergies); China Dolls; Breadcrumb Dolls; Blue Scarf Doll; Clothespin Dolls; Magic Hand Doll (picks up objects by means of a magnet hidden in its hand); Growing Doll (there are springs inside so its height can be increased); Magic Skin Doll (feels like human skin); Baby Skates (it skates); Saucy Walker (it walks); Punch and Judy Dolls (early versions were banned by the Catholic Church for becoming an entertainment medium rather than "teachers" of religion, and a Punch was ordered "executed," and the dolls were actually forbidden in England for one hundred years, for "criticising" Henry VIII); Wizard of Oz Dolls; Annie Rooney Dolls; Uncle Sam Dolls; Mickey Mouse Dolls; Sonja Henie Dolls; Aunt Jemima Dolls; Cream of Wheat Chef Dolls; Liberty Boy; Baby Ruth; Suckathumb Baby; Cracker Jack Baby; Zu-Zu Kid; Advertising Paper Dolls (touted McLaughlin's Coffee); Uneeda Biscuit Doll; Friendship Dolls (sent by American children to Japanese children); Alabama Baby; Columbian Sailor; Pitti-Sing; Topsy; Red Riding Hood Dolls; Our Soldier Boys Dolls; Dy-Dee; Kewpie; Scootles; Care Bears; Strawberry Shortcake Dolls; Star War Dolls; E.T. Dolls; Garfield Dolls; Snoopy Dolls; Mr. Potato Head; and, of course, Barbie.

Barbie is the top-selling doll of all time, with more than 200 million already having been purchased. There are almost as many Barbie dolls as there are people in the United States. First introduced in 1959, the dolls have been selling steadily ever since, and early versions are solid collectors' items, worth many times the original price. But in another sense it is not so surprising that so many Barbies have been sold: there are more dolls collectively on this planet than there are people.

Almost three million Cabbage Patch Kids were sold in 1983, surpassing by more than a million the previous first-year record, that of Baby Alive. Of course, the figures would have been even more impressive had Coleco been able to stay close to demand. Despite poor planning, the Cabbage Patch Kids demolished a record that not long before had seemed unapproachable.

"Nothing disappears quicker than today's shortages," says Bernie Loomis. He ought to know. Loomis once ordered an extra 110,000 Cheerful Tearful dolls for for his company, the highly successful Kenner, only to find that the craze had died and no one wanted them.

"That fate's almost certainly not in store for the Cabbage Patch Kids," wrote *Newsweek* magazine, December 12, 1983. "Coleco has already announced it will raise wholesale prices on the dolls at the end of the year. The company says it's only trying to recoup the extra cost of airlifting all those dolls from Hong Kong by Boeing 747s so they could be in their adoptive homes for the holidays. That piece of tinsel notwithstanding, Coleco is obviously hoping that the Kids will achieve the same classic status as Barbie, Ken, Raggedy and teddy — toys that sell all year long, year in and year out."

In a remarkably short time, the Cabbage Patch Kids have become enormously popular with collectors, who, said *Newsweek*, "look to the dolls more for cold, hard cash then soft, warm cuddles. Bennie and Jeannie Shelton of Cumming, Ga., who just laid out $5,000 to bring home a set of quintuplets, fully expect their darling infants to grow up into impressive capital gains. 'They are a tremendous investment,' boasts proud Papa Shelton."

The massive demand for Cabbage Patch Kids was created without tapping all of the potential of advertising. In fact, advertising had to be halted, because too great a demand had been elicited. Nor was full use made of the media. Xavier Roberts felt secure turning down an invitation to appear on the Johnny Carson Show, an invitation for which most promoters would kill.

Will the Cabbage Patch Kids reach the exalted status of Barbie, Raggedy Ann, and the teddy bear? Will they surpass in popularity the great sellers of all time?

There are many who think the Kids will, and the biggest reason may be that Coleco and especially Xavier Roberts, who even as a boy saw beyond the north Georgia mountains, understand that the appeal of dolls is universal. And the American people represent only a tiny portion (about six percent) of the earth's population.

8

Problems in Babyland

Just as the New Year of 1981 was being rung in, right at midnight, the New 'Ears Edition of Little People was being announced. There were 15,000 dolls in the edition, priced at $125 each. They were the first ever put out by Original Appalachian Artworks that weren't signed by Xavier. Instead his name was stamped on the dolls' behinds. This is the reason, perhaps, along with the fact that insufficient time has elapsed, that the New 'Ears Edition babies have not significantly increased in value. A baby from this edition is currently estimated to be worth $150.

The dolls in the New 'Ears Edition were unusual in that they were the first to have ears. The cause of this, Xavier explained with a straight face, was an error by a young intern. He had planted corn seeds too close to the newly planted cabbages. What else could the result be but New 'Ears?

Also in January, 1981, the first of the Unsigned "U" Edition was delivered to Babyland General Hospital. This edition would ultimately number more than 70,000, a tremendous amount for an expensive doll ($125) put out by a small town manufacturer. In fact, more than 70,000 dolls would have been impossible even to produce in the earlier days, when many of them were stitched in people's homes. "The Appalachian folks around here," says Xavier, explaining how he got started, "are very good at making things with their hands, so we paid them based on what they could produce in an hour. I've lived here all my life, so I knew practically everyone, and I also knew what they were capable of doing."

Now, however, there was a plant, a "top-secret" place "hidden" in a "mountain cabbage patch" where the babies were "born." It had to be this way. No matter how industrious the north Georgia residents were, they couldn't have produced in their homes the number of dolls Xavier intended to sell. And continuing as a cottage industry would have been utterly inconsistent with Xavier's plans for major success.

But 1981 was a year of deep recession in the United States. There had been double-digit inflation, which led to restricted credit and lessened buying power, which in turn led to accumulated stocks of goods, overproducing factories, canceled orders, dismissed workers, unemployment. Then the wheel turned again, in a more painful circle: further lessening of buying power, fewer markets, enforced sales at a loss, bankruptcies; a row of disastrous dominoes, each pushing down another in its fall. A major department store went belly-up. Tens of thousands of small businesses collapsed. Even banks went broke, and unemployment rose to alarming proportions.

Xavier was not immune to what was happening around him. In fact, he was in a business that was likely to be hurt the most.

In any society, there is a priority of needs which must be satisfied. Some products are essential to life and health, while others are not. The essentials are not difficult to list: food, water, medical care, housing, clothing, and in many instances electricity and/or gas, transportation, a telephone, a television, a newspaper, and supplies for school. Without many of these, life is difficult or impossible.

Then there are other goods, non-essentials, which make existence comfortable and even enjoyable. Among these are movies, cable TV, books, vacations, microwave ovens, vacuum cleaners, magazine subscriptions, health club memberships, dinners at restaurants, trips to ball games, visits to theaters, toys, and dolls.

If a child doesn't get a doll, he may whine or cry, but dinner can still be on the table.

The reason Xavier began to take a financial beating — "For awhile I was afraid we wouldn't make it," he says — is not complicated at all. Large portions of the consuming public could not afford a $125 doll. Being able to pay the heating bill,

CABBAGE PATCH DISPATCH
THE MAGAZINE FOR CABBAGE PATCH KIDS AND LITTLE PEOPLE COLLECTORS

OTIS LEE WANTS YOU

In depth interview with Presidential hopeful, Otis Lee.

CABBAGE PATCH DISPATCH
Spring 1983
$2.00

XAVIER ROBERTS INTRODUCES NEW COLLECTOR'S EDITIONS

DISPATCH
4 Years Old... Happy Birthday BabyLand!

CABBAGE PATCH DISPATCH
Summer 1983
$2.00
THE MAGAZINE FOR CABBAGEPATCH KIDS AND LITTLE PEOPLE COLLECTORS

SEE SUMMER TRAVEL GUIDE

BabyLand's Hottest Adoption Centers: How To Find Them When To Go What To Do

CABBAGE PATCH DISPATCH

• THE LEGEND OF THE LITTLE PEOPLE!
• INTERVIEW: XAVIER TALKS ON OTIS LEE!
• LITTLE PEOPLE AT THE WORLD'S FAIR!
• AND MUCH MORE!

EDITOR

Collector's Edition!

Volume 1 No. 1

PATCH DISPATCH
Volume 1 No. 2
$2.00

BABYLAND HITS THE BIG TIME!

INSIDE: Herschel Walker Interview!

Xavier's 90-room home in Cleveland, Georgia. A long way from the mobile home he lived in in the early days of business.

(Right) The pool and the slide, which is both functional as well as decorative. (Below) The hothouse. Eula could be seen on occasions here, "making things nice for Xavier." (Far Right) The grounds are dotted with color, either from flowers or from his growing car collection.

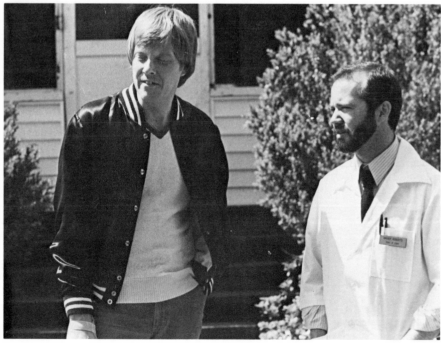

(Above Left) "This is crazy, even for our show!" (Left) Skip Stephenson and the young doctor Roberts. (Above) Sir Harold Wilson and Bette Midler adopt the Kids.

(Left) The faces only a mother could love, at the Easter Celebration given by Xavier in 1980. (Above) The only set of quintuplets ever delivered at Babyland. (Below) An adopting couple taking the oath.

Xavier and his Cabbage Patch Kids. His Kids remain quite different from Coleco's version (far page).

(Left) Heads of the Cabbage Patch Kids are packed in a box before they are assembled in a Hong Kong factory. Martin Bradfon and his attorney file a $100 million class action to stop the issuance of adoption papers. He did not prevail. (Below) Hong Kong workers inspect the dolls before packaging.

Paula Osborne, President
of Original Appalachian
Artworks, is responsible
for the Coleco mass
market deal as well as for
licensing the other off-
shoots coming from
Babyland.

Xavier is exploring new art forms.
These free-form sculptures in clay are an
example of what he calls "weed pots."

Many people adopt the Kids for investment as collectibles rather than for playthings alone. (Overleaf) Xavier and Otis Lee. Celebrities in their own land.

the food bill, the rent, all had become a question mark instead of a period for increasing numbers of citizens. Adopting a Little Person, as Xavier sadly learned, was hardly a high-priority item.

The fact that the very rich could still buy was of slight help. The rich were outnumbered by doctors whose patients could no longer afford to pay their bills, and thus the doctors had to cut back on their own consumption; by engineers who saw drawing board plans scrapped for lack of financing; by auto workers and steel workers who, if not already laid off, had to worry about their jobs and factories relocating to the Sun Belt; and, yes, by minimum-wage fast food clerks and struggling single mothers who also knew the anxious tug on the pants leg from the child who yearns for a cuddly doll but suspects correctly that it cannot be afforded.

As sales began to fall off, and orders suddenly to be cancelled, and reorders falling far short of expectations, Xavier increased personal energies that already bordered on the superhuman. Sixteen-hour workdays became twenty. He had never had trouble turning his ambition into productive labor, and now he worked as a man possessed. Surely, he thought, that was the solution to everything. He and a few others had built Original Appalachian Artworks from nothing, it had been a thrilling, exhilarating ride, and it was just not acceptable that it should end. But Xavier was caught in an economic iron vise, trapped by economic laws as strong, uncaring, and immutable as a great rock.

The situation at one point became so serious for the young Georgia entrepreneur that he came within minutes of not being able to meet a payroll. It was one of those countdown dramas where the hero — in this case a deliverer of money — doesn't arrive until the train is bearing down remorselessly on the helpless damsel.

What saved Original Appalachian Artworks, in the long run, was the upturn in the economy. The recession had driven Jimmy Carter from office, and the Reagan Administration, pumping dollars at a record rate into the economy, managed to reverse the trend. The prime rate dropped from 16.5% to 10.5%. Conventional home mortgages fell to 12.9%, down from 17.5%. The cost of new car loans dipped spectacularly. The logjam of money availability was broken, and the American people were able to spend again.

Economists had been telling people all along that the way to cure the recession was to spend more — advice similar to telling a drowning man to get out of the water. He most certainly would if he could. The pouring of money into the economy, like tossing a lifejacket to a drowning victim, accomplished what the spend-and-spend-more urgings could not.

Xavier's business teetered precariously close to the brink of disaster before the national economy improved and made life once again a happy, prosperous procession of gurgles around Babyland General Hospital. The early days of doing without, of Sharon Payne (now Sharon Mauney) and Xavier having to pledge their personal cars as collateral for a loan, now seemed part of an idyllic, trouble-free past. Perhaps this was because there was now so much more to lose. Even later, in a healthier fiscal posture, the doll maker would enjoy reminiscing about the past, as he did with Robert L. Shook, author of *Why Didn't I Think Of That!* "Boy, I'll never forget that first Chicago gift show. We got hit by a real good blizzard. We made expenses, but that's only because we really hustled. Yeah, hustling is the name of the game. We could have gone up there and sat around and let the buyers go past. But we didn't. We'd grab them and just let them have it! That's really what it takes, because although we have a great product, it's expensive. So we'd just pull them over to our booth and show them our babies.

" 'Do you mean to tell me this doll will sell for this price?' some people would ask."

" 'No, they don't *sell*,' we'd answer, smiling. 'This is the *adoption fee*. Then we'd show them our birth certificates and adoption papers, and before you knew it the buyers would be hooked."

Whatever else life was at Babyland General, it wasn't dull. Most businesses grind along in unchanging anonymity. People barely are aware they exist, and usually don't care. But Appalachian Artworks, Xavier, and the Little People were such a good story that they continued to attract media attention not just for themselves but for tiny Cleveland. On February 8, 1981, Xavier and his dolls were seen on ABC-TVs "World

News Tonight," with Xavier calling his product a "coffee break" from the exhausting routine of everyday life. If licensing agent Roger Schlaifer and Xavier were to arrange some sort of package deal with a major company, the type of exposure "World News Tonight" and "Real People" provided would make their bargaining position that much more solid. They could rightly claim the Little People were already well known, not nameless waifs who would have to be promoted from scratch.

Throughout all of this, before Xavier hit the big time with Coleco, he demonstrated a remarkable mixture of self-promotion and business acumen. Many hopeful entrepreneurs are skilled in one or two of these areas, but rarely both, and more often it is in the less important of the two, self-promotion. If a gimmick is unusual or bizarre enough (witness certain rock groups) the individual can promote himself, but there has to be a solid business base and a worthwhile product also. Xavier excelled at self-promotion — he merely had to be himself, a shy, dreamy spinner of pleasant fairy tales — and through sheer grit and determination he taught himself business expertise.

"I learned to ask for what I want," Xavier told the author. "I try to be firm in negotiations. There's no need to be friendly beforehand. The time for that is when the deal has been made."

About this time Xavier found himself in demand for various charitable affairs, and he helped whenever he could. He regarded the functions differently, as any sensible person would, from requests he later would receive from various politicians looking for campaign contributions. The latter, as any person who has achieved a degree of wealth and fame will attest, are as inevitable as broken campaign promises. But in any case, the charity affairs were usually for praiseworthy causes, and often Xavier was willing to lend a hand. His motivations undoubtedly were the highest — most of the fundraisers involved helping children, to whom he seems genuinely attached — but he was shrewd and perceptive enough to realize also that well-publicized appearances could only improve his image and that of his company.

One such charity benefit was at the Northeast Georgia

Medical Center in Gainesville for the dedication of a nursery, and Xavier pulled out all the stops. There probably had never been so many Little People congregated in one place at one time than on this occasion outside of Babyland General Hospital on the surrounding grounds. Xavier brought some of them with him, but so did parents from all over the area, eager to meet the young north Georgia celebrity. They also wanted Xavier to autograph their babies. Others adopted babies, with profits going to the clinic's Romper Roof, a pediatric playground. In addition, a Little Person was raffled off, and everyone who brought a doll to the dedication had it given a thorough physical examination by members of the Babyland General staff.

Another charity that sought and received assistance from Xavier was the Muscular Dystrophy Association. The event took place in Atlanta's Chastain Park; it was called Little People Parents Day, and hundreds of entrants took part in a costume contest, the first prize being an all-expense-paid trip for two to Disney World. Other prizes included numerous Little People, one of them a Grand Edition ($1,000) baby. Otis Lee was positioned near Xavier who sat under a massive cluster of brightly colored balloons signing autographs, and the Staff Stork, ever a popular figure, was on hand to pose for pictures.

Xavier went further with the Muscular Dystrophy Association than merely making a public appearance and giving away some babies. He ran the following advertisement, which speaks for itself.

HELP JERRY'S KIDS!

Hey, gang, if you want to do your part
to help stamp out Muscular Dystrophy *and*
get a great-looking tee-shirt in the
bargain, now's your chance! Each shirt
is of top quality construction, emblazoned
with the logo: "The Little People Help
Jerry's Kids." Proceeds from the sale of
these shirts will go to the Muscular
Dystrophy Association. So come on . . .
let's do what we can to help Jerry's kids!

The recession was continuing, and there were stirrings of fear at Babyland General Hospital, but that didn't stop the publicity. On April 12, 1981, Xavier was featured in a nine-page story in *Atlanta Weekly*, Sunday magazine of the *Atlanta Journal-Constitution*, the largest daily newspaper in the South. The highlight of the article was numerous pictures of Xavier's colossal house, replete with arches, chandeliers, mirrored walls, and fountains. A wooden bridge connected the main house with the guest quarters, and wherever the eye traveled it found potted plants, greenery dangling from rope hangings, a profusion of flowers. The foliage, largely tended by Eula, was lush and luxuriant.

A few steps after entering Xavier's house, the visitor is confronted by the swimming pool, and to the right and up above are more rooms than many hotels possess. The Little People are scattered everywhere, lounging in a lifelike setting, waiting to be autographed. Always an employee is nearby to remind Xavier of the autographing. He winces, smiles resignedly. But there are *so many of them.* One wonders what it would be like to sleep in this huge home, surrounded by dolls their creator claims are alive. But the dolls more than anyone belong here. They and their enterprising originator paid for the home.

Outside of course was the collection of classic cars, symbols of success, and possibly, like Xavier's babies, future collectibles whose value would increase. There was an MG, a vintage silver Jaguar, and two Mercedes. Not yet purchased was the Cadillac Seville limousine that would sport "XR-1" license plates and feature a Sony TV, stereo console, sun roof, and wet bar. This would be a "working" automobile, chauffeur-driven for Xavier and the increasing numbers of influential businessmen who had never heard of Cleveland, Georgia, before, but soon would come calling, briefcases in hand, to try to cash in on one of the hottest items in American merchandising history.

What the businessmen found inside Babyland General Hospital was impressive indeed, once they got in, but the area around the birthplace of the Little People was anything but imposing. Across the narrow side street is an Ace Hardware store. Just a few blocks away is the modest White County High

School, not yet bearing monuments to its most famous graduate.

The Cadillac Seville is driven by Dr. (not really) Jerry London. Actually, Jerry London turns out to be more than a chauffeur, or even an ersatz doctor, though he could have been mistaken for the real thing in his white smock. He is a trained, highly skilled magician, and along with fellow magician Robin Davis conducted regular magic show performances at Babyland General Hospital. One of their favorite tricks is to plunge a long, fearsome looking needle through a balloon, while children hold their ears waiting for the "pop!" that never comes.

"Every surgeon at Babyland," says Robin Davis to her audience, "has to take this test before they can work here. This is how we know if they are gentle enough."

She pauses. "But you have to be very careful," she says, pulling the needle all the way through the balloon, "because it's easy to make a mistake." Then she pokes the needle into the balloon again, exploding it and catching everyone by surprise.

"How did you do the balloon trick?" a child asks Robin Davis when the performance is over.

"Ask him," she says, pointing at a Cabbage Patch Kid dressed up in a magician's top hat and tuxedo. Then Robin Davis looks around, laughing. "That's what I like about working with the babies," she says. "They don't tell your secrets."

Jerry London was skilled at delivering Cabbage Patch Kids by what really was magic from a "patch" inside Babyland General Hospital. It was a show worth seeing. London would reach inside the patch and presto! pull out a newborn baby. "The deliveries are magic," he said, obviously enjoying his work. "The babies magically come to life, so this is a perfect tie-in with the enchantment that is already part of Babyland and evident everywhere you go here."

Babyland General Hospital, even the most avid critic of the Cabbage Patch Kids would admit, is a unique gift shop. It is better described as a children's wonderland with a hospital and playground decor than it is a business establishment. Not just the Cabbage Patch Kids are for sale, but stuffed animals of every variety, cards, clothes, books, toys, and records. But the hospital environment is the first and most lasting impression.

There are incubators occupied by Preemies. Supply rooms stuffed with baby food, baby oil, talcum powder, crib sheets, and diapers. A waiting room for fathers, who will receive a cigar whose wrapper announces "It's a boy!" or "It's a girl!" if he adopts a baby. An emergency room. Offices for doctors. Offices for nurses. A reception desk. Feeding room. Recess room. A delivery room where nurses wear "surgical masks." There is even a nursery school for the "older" Cabbage Patch Kids.

"One thing we do," Xavier told author Robert Shook, "is let our imaginations work to give each baby an individual personality, and we teach our shop owners how to do the same. When a prospective parent is browsing around the store, an on-the-ball adoption agent might point out a particular baby. 'Oh, that's Otis Lee in the corner. He's been a very bad boy today.' Or she might say, 'Faith Caroline has a tummyache today. Here, if you pick her up and rest her head on your shoulder, I'm sure she'll feel much better.' Then the adoption agent might add, 'How about burping Faith Caroline while I check on Otis Lee?'"

Said Xavier, a man with proof his ideas work, "It's just a matter of time before you automatically think and talk like this, and once you do, it's amazing how soon other people will react the same way. Sure, people will give you strange looks at first, but within ten minutes they catch on and they're doing the same thing and really enjoying it."

One of the areas it seemed natural for Xavier to branch into was book publishing. Walt Disney, a man for whom Xavier has unlimited respect, had made fortunes with comic books, comic strips, even regular books, and the young Georgian believed this area held bright possibilities for him also. Plaid Publishing, Inc., came out with his *Xavier Roberts Presents Little People Pals*, a 32-page book. Demonstrating chutzpah, Xavier had the book reviewed in the *Cabbage Patch Dispatch* by a Cabbage Patch Kid named Billy Badd.

This reviewer has read quite a few books in his time, and that's a fact. Some of them were very good books. Some were very bad books. Some of the books (usually the best ones) had pictures. Some needed pictures, and didn't have them. But never have I picked up a book that had as many things going for it as this new one from Plaid Publishing does.

For one thing, it has pictures and plenty of them. Color, too. To my way of thinking, a book without pictures is like a day without sunshine, and on that criterion alone, I can heartily recommend this work as a bright light shining out in the literary darkness.

For another thing, this book is positively oozing with drama. It artfully relates the legend of the Little People, bringing them to life with a rare sensitivity and attention to detail; qualities sadly lacking in most of today's run-of-the-mill potboilers. The book also examines the life and times of Xavier Roberts, designer with a no-bounds imagination whose creative artistry is clearly evident in each and every Little Person.

Particularly the handsome ones.

Finally, in what is surely one of the most poignant climaxes ever committed to type, the book illustrates — through the use of step-by-step instructions and even *more* pictures — how you, too, can make a Little People Pal for your very own. There is even a handy pattern included for your convenience, along with an official certificate authenticating it as a Xavier Roberts-designed doll!

This monumental work is, in short, as stunning a masterpiece as this reviewer has yet seen. Move over, Hemingway. Step aside, Faulkner. Make way for . . . the Little People Pals!

It might have seemed strange, in light of what would happen later, that Xavier printed "step-by-step instructions" on how to make a Little People Pal. When the Cabbage Patch Kids became a national phenomenon, it appeared at times to Xavier-watchers that he had as many lawsuits as Little People. Infringement would become for the young artist a problem of massive concern.

"Xavier Roberts," *Business Week* magazine wrote, "the

Georgia entrepreneur who owns the rights to the Cabbage Patch Kids, scored a life-size success with his dolls. But now his attorneys are launching a legal offensive to try to keep control of the wild market the product created. Roberts' problems — and the solutions his lawyers are mapping out — mirror those of many companies that exploit the public's increasing taste for heavily promoted brand-name merchandise.

"The more successful a marketing campaign, the more attractive it becomes for competitors to skirt the edge of copyright and trademark laws or to make outright illegal copies of an originator's line. Toymakers around the world — from a seamstress in Atlanta to shadowy industrial counterfeiters in the Far East — are turning out imitations of Roberts' pudgy-faced creatures."

Stanley F. Birch, Jr., one of Xavier's lawyers, estimated that the number of counterfeit Cabbage Patch dolls on the way to the United States was in the hundreds of thousands. Said William H. Needle, another of Xavier's attorneys, "We become aware of more infringements every day." The lawyers have even hired private investigators to search out the counterfeiters. "This is stealing," said Stanley Birch. "I think people need to understand that."

Even before the licensing agreement with Coleco, Xavier experienced problems. His lawyers won or settled eight cases before the Cabbage Patch Kids came into existence. But it was when the dolls became the object of frantic desire by consumers that the really serious difficulties arose. Stanley Birch, warning any potential counterfeiters, stated their position emphatically, "You'd better have enough capital to defend a lawsuit, because we're going to bring one against you."

There have been a spate of cases. Two men in New York were arrested and charged with copyright infringement, a misdemeanor punishable by up to one year in prison and a $25,000 fine. Attorneys for the defendants criticized federal authorities for basing the charges on the word of a private investigator who said he went undercover and bought allegedly counterfeit dolls for $12 each.

But this case was relatively small potatoes. In Chicago, postal authorities swooped down on a man running ads guaranteeing Cabbage Patch Kids to anyone sending him $19.50. The postal service said the accused couldn't produce a single one.

What concerned Xavier and Coleco most, however, was that a big manufacturer would produce a doll "substantially similar" to the Cabbage Patch Kids and begin to mass-market it. They were aware that probably thousands of cottage industries had grown up based on the Kids, with housewives stitching Cabbage Patch look-alikes at a fevered pace, mostly doing nothing more than earning a few extra dollars. People at Coleco were well aware of the Cabbage Patch underground but, as a spokesman for the company said, they "can see the headlines now" if they tried to stop it.

The news accounts would surely have been unfavorable, especially during the 1983 Christmas Madness, largely caused by Coleco's slick promotion, when the company itself couldn't keep dolls in the stores. Prosecuting a grandmother or an enterprising housewife stitching dolls out of her home was not the kind of publicity Xavier or Coleco needed. Both seemed to understand this very well. As long as the underground versions were not called Cabbage Patch Kids, it was likely they could be made on a small scale with impunity.

In May, 1981, the Second Preemie Edition was introduced at Babyland General, 10,000 babies selling for $130 each (current estimated market value $150). These dolls were stamped, not autographed, and came attired in pastel-colored designer christening gowns. In keeping with the premature theme, the adoption papers and birth certificates were produced in miniature. The Preemies, it was originally explained, were the result of "a blackberry winter." There would be explanations much more ingenious for other editions.

The Oriental Edition, for example, "imported" from the "Far Eastern" side of the Cabbage Patch, came about because "a large amount of bokchoy was sprinkled among the cabbages by accident." A Babyland General Hospital announcement claimed that "The occurrence of a crop of Oriental babies in the Patch came as somewhat of a surprise to the doctors and nurses at Babyland, who had to quickly send out for a shipment of chopsticks and tea to replace the less exotic pacifiers and milk normally stocked in the hospital nursery."

The American Indian Edition, 500 "chiefs" and 500 "maidens," were clad in authentic costumes. The boys wore "mohawk" hairstyles, the girls had long dark braids, and they came dressed in moccasins and beads. According to Babyland General, the dolls were the result of a late — or "Indian" — summer in the Cabbage Patch.

In June, 1981, for the first time in almost four years, a Standing Edition was released. There were five thousand of these babies, adopting out for a hefty $300 each (estimated value now $350). These dolls, 23 inches tall, resembled toddlers and came in fashions specifically designed by Xavier. Again the dolls were stamped, not personally autographed, and stood with faces upturned and arms outstretched, a pose that seems to prompt people to pick the babies up and hug them.

The nation was sunk deep in a recession now, and it is doubtful if there could have been a Cabbage Patch Craze in 1981. In hindsight, Xavier was probably lucky he didn't meet up with Coleco earlier. "Being in the right place at the right time" is an overused cliché often applied to Xavier, but like many other clichés it rings true. When the big Northern company and the young Southern artist did finally get together, the time was right. The big question up to that point was whether the brutal economic slump, striking hardest at "soft" goods like Xavier sold, would drive Xavier out of business before he could make the big score.

In July, 1981, ground was broken for a new addition to Babyland General. When it was completed, the gift shop truly was like no other in the world. A Little People Hall of Fame marked the entrance to the new section, and from there a visitor crosses a footbridge over a pond and enters a world of plants, mirrors, waterfalls, Cabbage Patch Kids everywhere, and a kaleidoscope of sight and sound that surprises and excites. Storks look almost alive, a giant stuffed tiger is crouched to pounce, bears hold Cabbage Patch Kids, and vice versa.

The new addition was aptly named "Another World." It occupied 4,500 square feet and included a petting zoo (soft sculpture animals only), a party room, and a fish pond. There was even a place to throw a birthday bash for your Little Person. It was called the Little People Birthday Room, and it came complete with party favors, balloons, hats, and streamers.

A member of the group Xavier calls "Cabbagesseurs" — collectors who specialize in the Little People — is Dorothy For-ward of Stone Mountain, Georgia, who adopted her first baby in 1981, and a year later had twenty-seven of them. Mrs. For-ward expressed the feelings of her daughter Judy and her hus-band Roy when the initial baby made its appearance. "Judy and I were crazy about the baby — a New 'Ears girl — as soon as she was brought home. But Roy was not totally convinced about this new addition to the family. He's a banker and was a little unsure about the expense.

"During a visit to Savannah, however, we chanced upon Hugh Sterling, a Bronze Edition baby. It was at this time that we really understood how valuable and collectible the Little People are, and this is what finally brought Roy around."

A year later, the Forwards had at least one baby from each edition. Their collection included what Babyland General Hospital describes as "two very glamorous celebrities," the King of Siam and Anna.

"Even so," said Dorothy Forward, "we have no favorites. We enjoy every one of our Little People in a different way, because every one has a different personality. I guess that's why we have adopted so many babies. We know that they are a unique work of art, and therefore are collectible and valuable . . . but we love them for their personalities."

Another example of Cabbagesseurs was the Klein family — parents David and Carol and daughters Laurie, Cheryl, and Deanna — of Albuquerque, New Mexico. They adopted their first baby July 7, 1981, at the Decatur, Georgia, Babyland Clinic while on a side trip from visiting friends in Atlanta. "Ruth Trixie picked me out in thirty seconds," said Carol Klein. Slightly more than a year later the Kleins had forty-five Little People!

"We have babies from almost all the limited editions," said Carol Klein, "as well as several Pals. One of the babies even has the same name and birthday as mine."

Laurie and Cheryl, college students, took their babies with them to school. David, described by his wife as the most ag-gressive in the family, said his baby was aspiring to be a major league baseball player. "We fell in love with the babies," said Carol, "because of their personalities and the enjoyment of their surrounding fantasy, and really just have begun to consider the investment aspect of them. In fact, we consider every Little Person we meet as a valuable creation."

Georgia Frontiere, owner of the Los Angeles Rams, might even be considered a Cabbagesseur. She gave out more than one hundred Cabbage Patch Kids to players on her team after last season's playoff game with the Washington Redskins. The Rams were humiliated in the contest, 51-7, by a team that also had a Cabbage Patch connection. Super-fan Frances Bernhard dressed two of her Cabbage Patch Kids in Washington jerseys to bring luck to the Redskins.

Incidentally, according to the Rams public relations director, Pete Donovan, "It took us over three weeks to round up those hundred dolls."

On July 22, 1981, in an exclusive interview with the *Chicago Tribune*, Xavier announced the introduction of doctor and nurse outfits that could be purchased for Little People, and also — to be ready by fall — a line of Xavier Roberts designer jeans. Always there were new vistas, new merchandise to bring out, new markets to explore, for because the Little People were endowed with the gift of life, their needs could be as broad as humanity itself. Xavier wondered why the world couldn't be made to love his babies. He had foreseen that their popularity would stretch far beyond north Georgia. Why not across oceans?

A group of Babyland nurses traveled to Paris, France, in October, 1981, to test the marketing waters in one of the world's most cultured cities. The nurses received a "curious acceptance," as one can easily imagine, according to Original Appalachian Artworks own assessment.

In November, 1981, Xavier himself was off to the Orient for a month, ostensibly to look for exotic gift items for Another World, soon to open, but also to check the reactions the Little People received. Throughout history the great dolls of the world possessed appeal that was international, and the young Georgian believed all that was required to love his babies was to know them. Xavier traveled to Korea, Taiwan, Hong Kong, the Philippines, and Japan. As a little boy a trip as far as Atlanta would have been undreamed of; as a young man he would circle the globe.

And Xavier was right in believing his dolls could successfully cross international borders. In February, 1984, an American visitor to Japan might have thought he was suffering an extreme case of déjà vu. The Land of the Rising Sun experienced its own version of Cabbage Patch Madness. Retailers in Tokyo reported that the first batch of Cabbage Patch Kids was snatched up immediately by eager customers, with many would-be buyers returning home disappointed.

The Cabbage Patch Kids sold for 6,500 yen each ($28), had Japanese names, and of course came with adoption papers and birth certificates.

It really did remind one of what happened in the United States. In a scramble to be among the first in Japan to adopt a Cabbage Patch Kid, a large crowd started lining up outside Takashimaya Department Store's Nihonbashi Shop at 6 A.M. Only three thousand dolls were part of this first consignment, though a spokesman for Tsukuda Original, the Japanese agent for the babies, predicted sales would top 500,000 in 1984.

Part of the reason for going overseas was not just to find markets for more dolls he could manufacture, but to locate homes for those he already had produced. The big Reagan tax cuts, deficits, and expanded defense spending had not yet produced their effects on the economy. People *had* to eat, and somehow find money for mortgages. They did *not* have to buy expensive dolls.

Before they became a happy reality, Xavier had long suspected that profits from other nations would provide a rich icing on top of his American cake. Five hundred thousand dolls in a single year in Japan alone! There were more than 150 countries out there, and the young Georgian couldn't imagine a one that wouldn't hunger for his babies if given half a chance. France and England have already become major markets. Even Israel seems likely to succumb. "How about the Soviets?" Xavier was asked. "Will your babies adopt in the Soviet Union?"

"That would be something," he says. "We'd love to take the Kids to Russia. But, no, I don't think they're interested right now."

The agent for the Cabbage Patch Kids in Japan, Tsukuda, suffered the exact criticism Coleco had experienced earlier. Consumer advocates charged that Tsukuda had deliberately created a shortage.

Cabbage Patch Kids did not sell well in Hong Kong, though the reason was not a lack of popularity. The price of $195 H.K. ($25 U.S.) effectively priced them out of most people's reach. Workers in Hong Kong's toy factories average about $7.70 U.S. a day.

Before the Japanese proved that Americans weren't alone in their willingness to stand in long lines for hours (though theirs was of the *non*violent ilk), Bob Hope was cracking jokes about the craze that had gripped the United States. "If you think you guys are fighting over here," Hope told an audience of marines at Beirut Airport, "you should see them battling for Cabbage Patch dolls back home."

The New York Department of Consumer Affairs did not find the Christmas Madness amusing and took action, something which has not occurred yet in Japan. Declaring that the demand for Cabbage Patch Kids "far exceeds the supply or the ability of the manufacturer to make and deliver to the retailer in time for the holidays," the Department of Consumer Affairs warned: "Our office now has inspectors in the field in an attempt to monitor sales of this item, and to be sure that retailers are not advertising this product without a certain number to supply the anticipated demand. 'Bait and Switch' and 'Come-on' gimmicks will not be tolerated on this unusually strong seller."

Xavier managed to remain above the thunderbolts of criticism that accompanied the Madness of 1983, and indeed whatever shortcomings appeared in the marketing strategy (and these were many), they did not seem traceable to him. Coleco was the one which underestimated the market. The creator of the Cabbage Patch Kids never doubted that his babies would become every bit as popular as they did. While Coleco tried to field hostile questions from consumer groups and adoption organizations, Xavier became an internationally feted celebrity, humbly acknowledging his success and attributing it all to hard work. One thing he refused to do. Those who interviewed him dearly wanted an acknowledgement that his success had come as a surprise. Didn't the rags-to-riches, up-from-the-bottom young mountain man find it all a great deal amazing? "No," he always replied. He had expected it. And so, he could have added, had his mother, Eula. One Cleveland resident, hearing that a book titled *Fantasy* was being planned, decided "That's a word that applies to more than just people believing the dolls are real. That boy and his mother were poor. Dirt poor, even by the standards around here. But they were talented. Look at the beautiful work that woman could do. And Xavier was talented. And both the mother and son had imaginations. I think they lived in a fantasy world where everything turned out all right in the long run. That's what I would have done in their situation. How else do you stand what life's given you? Maybe I'm way off, a know-nothing amateur psychologist, but I believe their fantasy became so lifelike they thought it had to come true." And it was a fantasy that others happily shared.

9

The Adoption Controversy

Concerned United Birthparents (CUB), a nationwide support group for parents who give up their children to adoption, launched a campaign against the Cabbage Patch Kids, and was joined by pro-adoption groups in New Jersey and Canada. Said CUB President Lee Campbell: "They advertise them as kids, not dolls. They come with a birth certificate. They have adoption papers. Each one is a little different from the others." Kathy Sawyer, a regional coordinator for CUB in Plano, Texas, gave up her own child for adoption. "It was the single most hurtful experience in my life," says Mrs. Sawyer, "and I resent people taking it so lightly."

CUB first became concerned about the Cabbage Patch Kids in March, 1983, when members visited a Coleco booth at a gift show. There they witnessed a "doctor" delivering a "baby" from a "cabbage patch," handing it to a "nurse," who slapped the "baby" on the bottom, then delivered it to a "parent" for "adoption." "This was more than we could take," said Ms. Campbell, whose group promptly protested to Coleco.

In May, 1983, Coleco dispatched two representatives to discuss the complaint with CUB members. CUB suggested several alternatives, one being to change the phrase "adoption papers" to "parenting papers." But no changes were forthcoming. "They ignored us," said Ms. Campbell.

Criticism of the adoption gimmick came from all quarters. Toni Peters, president of the Dallas, Texas, Council on Adoptable Children, received numerous complaints from members of her group. "They say the Cabbage Patch Kids degrade the concept of adoption."

A different type of complaint was voiced by Tonya Harris of Chicago. "The money those people spend on dolls could feed a starving child somewhere for months. If they have so much love to give, they should give it to real children."

"One in four families in the United States," says Atlanta's Diane Brown, a charter member of the American Adoption Congress, "is affected by adoption in some way. Whenever there is an adoption, there is hurt on all sides. The people who make these adoption dolls are trading on an emotion. They could have clubs and things. But unless you walk in the shoes of someone else, you don't know how they feel."

Martin Brandfon of San Francisco took a different tack from other protestors. He filed a whopping $100 million class action lawsuit against both Coleco and Xavier, claiming that the marketing material used for the Cabbage Patch Kids is harmful to him and other adopted people.

The Christian Science Monitor quoted an individual described as an "adoption expert," who suggested there was a comparison between the selling of black-market babies (a big business in the U.S.) and the rioting, scalping, and attempts at bribery that marked the 1983 Christmas phenomenon. "Some white families are so desperate for babies, they are doing desperate things to be able to adopt one. The analogy with the dolls struck me deeply. It's very analogous and very destructive."

But the experts were divided. "I was a black-market baby originally," says Samuel Levine, executive director of the non-profit American Adoption Agency in Washington, D.C. Levine contends the Cabbage Patch Kids "may be a good opportunity to resolve some questions about adoption." And psychiatrist Kent Ravenscroft of the Children's Hospital in Washington, D.C., thought the Kids were "an exciting development," making the adoption process appear more natural.

A social worker in New York City's Children's Aid Society, Susan Silverman, who deals with adopted children every day, thought the adoption process was degraded by the marketing of the Cabbage Patch Kids. "In the current craze, the adopted dolls are treated like objects, not like babies to be cherished." But Jane Edwards, who heads up an adoption agency in New York City, saw the matter differently: "I've talked with several adoptive parents about the dolls, and they don't feel offended by them. I don't feel it trivializes adoption."

The issue really seemed to be an important one, with the Cabbage Patch Kids having touched an exposed nerve. A woman in New Hampshire said the marketing of the dolls suggested that adopted children "come from low-life vegetables — cabbages," and can be purchased just like a vegetable. Donna Light of Montpelier, Vermont, a CUB member, said "This desensitizes kids to the reality of adoption. There's pain and suffering in giving up a child."

But what is the truth? Jerry Cornez, national executive director of WAIF, an organization working with hard-to-place children, said he was "delighted" with the Cabbage Patch Kids precisely because they did come with adoption papers. "A lot of children who are adopted feel different because somebody gave them up. We feel that by educating kids through adopting a doll, taking care of it and being responsible for that doll, it tells the kids that families are formed in many different ways. We hope youngsters will feel special instead of different."

Certainly St. Luke's Hospital in Cedar Rapids, Iowa, didn't see any danger in the adoption process used by Xavier and Coleco. St. Luke's, because the demand for the Cabbage Patch Kids was not being met, sent out birth certificates for any type of doll. "We know children's babies are very real to them," said Myrt Bowers, vice president of nursing at the hospital. "When the Birthcare Center staff heard some children were being disappointed at not being able to adopt a certain brand of doll, we thought we could help a little and let them adopt any doll."

John Tepper Marlin, an adoptive parent from New York City, could see both good and bad in the marketing plan employed first by Xavier, then by Coleco. "The good feature of the dolls," said Marlin, "is that they indicate a healthy change in the public's attitude toward adoption. As recently as two decades ago, some adoptive parents didn't even tell their children they were adopted, as if adoption were something to be ashamed of. Children readily picked up messages like that." On the downside, said Marlin, "A child who can discard an 'adopted' doll when its novelty palls might conclude that adoptive parents are free to discard their adoptive child. Real adoption is different, above all because it is forever. What would the public reaction be to a 'child-bearing' mama doll, complete with a baby and snap-apart umbilical cord? Wouldn't most parents feel that the trivialization of birth outweighed the possible educational value of such a doll?"

Richard Schwarzchild, president of the advertising agency Coleco retained to promote the Cabbage Patch Kids, a man partly responsible for a campaign so successful that ads had to be pulled off the air, quite naturally thought the adoption process was a positive force for good. Nonetheless, what Schwarzchild has to say may have merit: "If you treated a Shirley Temple doll as if it were alive, people would treat you as if you were crazy. But because this is so ugly, it allows everybody to get into the fantasy that they are real."

Steven Kolker, senior vice president of the same advertising agency, agrees with Schwarzchild, then adds, "The key was understanding that kids also want to feel one-of-a-kind and say to themselves, 'No matter how I look, I'm special.' "

Interestingly, the Cabbage Patch Kids were called "dolls" in television ads. Coleco, Xavier, and the advertising agency — Richard & Edward — wanted to refer to them as "babies," but all three networks, fearing a hassle with the FCC and not eager to lend their names to what could be termed the unreal, adamantly refused.

Dr. Bruce Axelrod, a child psychologist and director of Comprehensive Mental Health Services in Milwaukee, Wisconsin, agrees with Steven Kolker, saying the adoption papers and the less-than-beautiful appearance of the Cabbage Patch Kids make it easier for youngsters to identify with them. "It's very difficult for most girls to feel that they look like the Barbie dolls. The Cabbage Patch Kids, on the other hand, are not so perfect, are not so attractive. This enables the average child to say, 'Hey, this could be me.' Most children between the ages of six and twelve fantasize that they were really adopted or were born to another set of parents and that they were mixed up in the hospital. Psychologically, this is a sign that the child is beginning to separate from the family, a necessary part of growing up. A child who adopts a Cabbage Patch Kid can act out the fantasy of being adopted. They can now play in play what they experience in fantasy."

Whatever the pros and cons of the adoption process Xavier initiated, the fact that it and the Cabbage Patch Kids drew so much attention from serious observers indicated the depth of the phenomenon and the impact it was believed to be having on American society. The eminent Dr. Lee Salk, professor of pediatrics and psychology at Cornell University Medical College, said the birth certificates and adoption papers "increased possessiveness, underscored children's identity with parents, and their need for a sense of belonging."

Heavy hitters, not just glib pop psychologists, found themselves fascinated by the popularity of the Cabbage Patch Kids, and the role played by the act of adoption. For instance, Dr. Malcolm W. Watson, associate professor of developmental psychology at Brandeis University stated, "The relative uniqueness of each doll, as well as the procedure of adopting the doll and committing to it, increase the child's ease of attachment to the doll and the use of it as a companion."

Dr. Paul C. Horton, author of *Solace*, a study of the need of humans for objects that provide comfort, said children "need attachments external to themselves to give solace and comfort," that a Cabbage Patch Kid "is a possession a child is instantly able to make his own," that "for younger children it is more than a doll," and "for older children the idea of adoption becomes compelling."

Dr. Esther Schaler Buchholz, a clinical psychologist and director of psychology of New York University's Parenthood Program, found the adoption procedures allowed children to "take on adult roles, to experience emotions and control them through a bond with the doll."

Whether or not the requiring of an oath of adoption and the entire notion that the Cabbage Patch Kids cannot be bought exercises a positive influence on children (and adults), no one for an instant should believe Coleco was unaware, *before* the dolls were even marketed, that it was wielding a powerful sales tool. The company did know that the idea would work, as surely as a pollster can measure public opinion through just a minuscule sampling of the population. Xavier first employed the procedure when he was torn between his need for money and his attachment to one of his works. He didn't want to part with the doll and resolved the problem through the method of adoption. By means of this fiction he considered that he really wasn't doing something as insensitive as selling an object which was dear to him. Xavier stumbled upon the adoption ploy by accident, almost like Newton being hit on the head by an apple, used it again, and when it worked again incorporated it into an everyday mode of doing business. What Xavier discovered was by luck. As will be seen, no luck at all was involved for Coleco.

The importance Xavier attached to the oath of adoption can be judged by written instructions given each adoption center with which he did business: "Solemnly ask the Adoptive Parent to raise their right hand and REPEAT THE OFFICIAL OATH OF ADOPTION after you. This is of great importance and should not be underestimated. Failing to give the Official Oath of Adoption could possibly result in the Adopting Parent not understanding the true commitment in becoming a Little Person Parent."

The birthday of a Cabbage Patch Kid is not the day he is manufactured into a single whole, but the day he is adopted. Adoption centers were told to fill out on the birth certificate not only the day of the sale, but the time. This spawned the illusion that the Cabbage Patch Kid had no past before being adopted, and also was easier for bookkeeping purposes. A copy of the adoption papers was returned to Babyland General Hospital, where the new parents became part of a mailing list. The date of the sale was used to determine when the first birthday card should be sent.

Besides the oath of adoption, there were *fifteen other steps* the adoption centers were urged to take during the adoption process.

Newsweek magazine, December 12, 1983, provided as good an explanation as any of why the fantasy of adoption was successful: "In all the commotion, there is no getting around the fact that Cabbage Patch Kids are ugly. But their ugliness has a touching runt-of-the-litter quality that adults and children alike find irresistible — a vulnerability that arises in part from their expression (which can be approximated in an adult face by sucking in both lips and puffing out the cheeks), eternally poised between a gurgle and a sob. After three years of toys with hearts of microchips, Cabbage Patch dolls address what child psychologist Doris McNeely Johnson calls 'a universal need that children have to hold something and cuddle it.' Without actually resembling any real baby that has ever walked the earth — for which the whole human race can be grateful — Cabbage Patch Kids caricature almost every characteristic of babiness: blunt, fat features; round cheeks; big eyes; short, pudgy little arms and legs.

"The Cabbage Patch press kit includes a paper by Brandeis University psychologist Malcolm Watson, who points out that these features constitute a 'releasing mechanism' that triggers the instinct for nurturing in both adults and children. The same powerful instinct, vital to the preservation of our species, that makes you want to pick up and hug a baby in his crib has been harnessed to make you want to snatch a $25 toy off the shelf. The notion that the Kids are 'adopted'— not just purchased — doubtless assists that release of protective love."

New York child psychologist Dr. Miriam Sherman offered a thought-provoking thesis. She says that while doll play is normal for young children, with adults it is usually a replacement for interaction with other human beings. "The dolls allow adults to become babies again," she says.

Xavier disagreed with the regression-into-infancy notion. "I don't think people dream nowadays," he says. "So I sell a little bit of imagination."

But to whom? Most parents during the Madness of 1983 said it was their children who insisted on having a Cabbage Patch Kid for Christmas, that little hearts would be broken if Santa failed to deliver. The truth is, however, that when Xavier started out, the vast majority of his sales were to mothers and grandmothers, seeing the dolls for the first time and adopting them without any consultation with children. And later, during what one newspaper called "Terror in Toyland," it seemed to most observers that older people were the ones who *had* to have the Cabbage Patch Kids.

Peter David, who works for the Marvel Comics Group, writing in *The New York Times*, agreed that the appeal of the dolls was largely to adults. "It is the parents of America who are acting like children, and spoiled brats at that. Convinced by the media, and by themselves, that the Cabbage Patch Kids are the only present worth giving this year ('Sally, you want a Cabbage Patch baby this year, don't you?') and being part of a society that has taught us to expect instant gratification, parents are incensed when they can't have the new toy immediately. They threaten, they stomp, they react in ways they would not tolerate from their own children.

"They are also terrified that failure to obtain one of the dolls will make them less of a parent. Terrified of losing face in their children's eyes, they are behaving in a way that is generally reserved for times of national crisis, all the while hiding behind a cloak of benevolence. 'It's for the kids' sakes,' we are told. How unselfish. But it's not the concern that their child might not get this toy for Christmas that has parents trembling. It's the thought that someone else's child might. After all, there was no overt concern when America's youth once got promissory notes for Star Wars figures in their stockings because of manufacturing delays."

Two nationally syndicated columnists, Dr. Joyce Brothers and Ellen Goodman, with Dr. Brothers the more enthusiastic, had something good to say about the Kids. "It is comforting," wrote Joyce Brothers, herself a psychologist, "to feel the Cabbage Patch doll can be loved with all your might — even though it isn't pretty." Ellen Goodman decided: "I am not sure that the Cabbage Patch fad means anything much except that advertising works. The doll itself has a kind of squishy, cutesy ugliness. Blessedly, it doesn't do anything, and has no batteries. It's a welcome relief from the biological dolls of a few years ago that performed every bodily function short of childbirth."

The *Dallas Morning News,* quoting Coleco's Barbara Wruck on the importance of the adoption ritual — "It solidifies the bond between the buyer and the Cabbage Patch Kid" — also found merit in what Ellen Goodman had mentioned: "But what seems to be an even better explanation for the craze is the product itself. Above all, it has simplicity. A Cabbage Patch Kid doesn't wet its pants or blink its eyes. It doesn't make any noise, have batteries to install or buttons to push."

"Other popular dolls," said Dr. William Tedford of Southern Methodist University, a psychology professor, "already have their personality built in. But it's about time for a plain baby doll that just lies there and lets a child mother it."

Much of the mania over the Cabbage Patch Kids was indeed a reaction to the increasing number of sophisticated toys that demanded from their owners a good deal of mechanical expertise but required very little imagination or attachment. Lifesize robots, for example, requiring what seemed to many the expertise of a professional mechanic merely to assemble, were not likely to be the sort of companion a child wished to cuddle and confide in, nor were electronic video games something with which a youngster could form a bond of warm friendship. Even the whiz kids (most of the advances are made by young people in their twenties, and these often "burn out" before they reach thirty) of our high tech, high speed, high pressure society become disoriented and bewildered by the uses they discover to which the new technology can be applied. In this light it is no wonder that children would call a halt, at least take a breath, before continuing at the dizzying pace, and fall in love with a doll that is a throwback to an era less hurried.

The fantasy of adoption, of course, naturally led children to ask their parents the names of the real mother and father of their Cabbage Patch Kids. The father was easy enough: the kindly Xavier Roberts. The name of the mother was often not so clear. But even this natural curiosity was something which might be turned to profit.

A little girl named Laura Mann wrote to Babyland General: "I'm the mother of Nan Felicia. Sometimes she wakes up in the night. What should I give her? Do you think she is a little homesick?"

Babyland General wrote back: "It's possible. Although Little People always love their new homes, they sometimes get to thinking about all the friends they left behind in the Cabbage Patch. You might consider taking Nan on a trip to Babyland General Hospital, where she will be able to visit with her friends for awhile. That should take care of the problem."

That the adoption process is a serious matter to certain prospective parents is undeniable. There are literally millions of people in the United States who have considered adopting a baby, and Cabbage Patch Kids actually have become an alternative for some of these. A Phoenix, Arizona, woman put it more bluntly than others might: "I can shower this baby with as much love, affection, and material goods as I want. And I can stop whenever I want also, and never hear a single complaint."

The birth certificates issued with the Cabbage Patch Kids created a situation that was both humorous and serious. Government officials complained that felons and illegal aliens were using the birth certificates to obtain Social Security cards. The birth certificates issued by Xavier were modeled after the real thing, but it was clearly a facsimile and could easily be spotted by anyone looking closely. It appeared certain government workers were gifted with less than eagle eyes.

A more serious problem arose when certain hospitals issued real blank birth certificates to "children" who had been unable to adopt a doll during the 1983 Christmas Madness. The "young people" turned out not to be young people, in many instances, and the birth certificates they obtained could be used for countless questionable purposes. A "significant number" of hospitals in the United States handed out birth certificates in this manner, according to Sterling, Illinois, Social Security official, John Burr, and this often meant that individuals possessing *real* certificates from these institutions could not use them as proof of identification.

In Summit County, Indiana, doll owners asked officials to register Cabbage Patch Kids, just as flesh-and-blood adopted children were registered. "Real adoptive parents," wrote the *Richmond* (Indiana) *Palladium Item*, "have enough problems explaining adoption to their youngsters without having to dispel rumors about birth in 'enchanted cabbage patches.' Some adults might find the dolls' instant adoption a painful contrast to the years they've waited to adopt a child." In the middle of the furor was state senator, David Nicholson, who introduced a bill in the Indiana General Assembly to allow adults, eighteen years of age and older, to look at their adoption files and original birth certificates. The legislation was opposed by parents who had put their children up for adoption and did not want their children to learn their roots.

Anti-abortion individuals even got into the act, attempting to contrast the adoption of the Cabbage Patch Kids and the characteristic fuss made over them to the "lack of concern" shown for the unborn. A writer to the *Suffolk County* (New York) *News* asked, "So why with all this interest and mania, do we allow real babies or 'kids' to be aborted by the thousands in this country? Why do we allow abortion groups to call these *real* kids fetuses or embryos? These are real kids with real human qualities, with life. They come in different races, would have different names. They're not manufactured but *born* to us, each one a gift, every day of the year. They're not a fad for the holidays. They possess something other than life; they possess love and the ability to love us back."

"Some people have been conditioned to justify abortion in the same way some have been conditioned to accept Cabbage Patch Kids as real. We must all stand up and see the outrage which is happening in this country."

The adoption papers, and the fantasy that Cabbage Patch Kids were babies, was carried to new lengths of the fantastic in Yonkers, New York, where a "Cabbagetizing" ceremony took place. According to that city's *Herald Statesman,* "The idea originated with Connie Santuzzi whose little girl, Lisa, was given a Kid as a gift. After checking the doll over and noting that even the belly button was intact along with a birth certificate stating parentage, she thought it would be a good idea if the doll were baptized. So on Monday, 'Sherwood,' dressed in the very same outfit Lisa wore for her baptismal, and all the other Kids who show up, will be Cabbagetized. A Godmother and Godfather will be available and you'll also receive a certificate noting the occasion."

A more serious aspect of the adoption question was addressed by well known child psychologist Marilyn Machlup in the *Cincinnati Call and Post.* "Many young children imagine that they are adopted as a way to cope with their disappointments about their parents' ways of handling them. They imagine that, somewhere in the world, they have ideal parents who would always please them, never say 'no' to them, and provide all the splendors of living. To 'adopt' a Cabbage patch doll, the child may play out the fantasy of being adopted from the security of knowing all along that he is found."

Marilyn Machlup went on. "There is a myth about the origin of babies that comes to us from Western Europe. The myth is that babies are found in cabbage patches, thus doing away with the sexuality of pregnancy and birth. While young children are curious about their bodies, its functions and about their own origins, they find this information difficult to process — to understand and accept. They take many years to come to a full understanding and acceptance of the way it is, sexually."

After pointing out that children are more comfortable when their sexuality develops "at its own pace and time," Ms. Machlup concluded that "The Cabbage Patch Kids are a breath of fresh air in a too exciting and excitable world. Our children need all the help we can give them to remain calm and in control of themselves as they play, learn and grow." But there were arguments on all sides of the adoption question. "Some of the individuals I've talked with," said South Carolina psychologist Murray Chesson, "did have negative connotations about going into a store and buying another individual, and about owning another person."

Three men in Myrtle Beach, South Carolina, decided to find out how much people would pay for the hard-to-get dolls. "As a joke" and "an experiment in human psychology," they offered a "twin set" of Cabbage Patch Kids for the "best offer over $2,000." "We were sitting around one day," said Harry Chambers, "talking about this nutty thing with Cabbage Patch dolls and how people were flying around the world buying these ugly things. . . . We thought we'd perform our own experiment in human nature. We wanted to make it difficult to get these dolls to see how far people will go. Who knows, somebody may be stupid enough to fall for this."

No readoption was arranged, though several people did call. "I don't think they had the right pocketbook," said Harry Chambers. "They asked too much about the price. If they had to do that, they aren't interested in our precious ugly dolls."

It was Murray Chesson, the South Carolina psychologist, who pointed out a decision Xavier already knew he would have to make. If children were allowed to play with Cabbage Patch Kids, their popularity would likely continue. If the Kids were promoted as "objects of art" and employed chiefly for display purposes, the public interest would quickly fade.

A New York fourth grade teacher, Sally La Valle, asked her students to describe what it would be like to be a Cabbage Patch Kid. The results buttressed Xavier's contention that fantasy played a big role in the appeal of his creations.

"I'm a Cabbage Patch doll," wrote one little girl. "All the people go crazy over me. Many people want to take me home with them."

"I want someone to be my guardian," wrote a second little girl. "I sat for weeks and weeks alone. A sad little girl stopped and looked at me. Her mommy paid for me and brought me home. The little girl gave me lots of tender love and care."

In Fort Worth, Texas, there was even a legal adoption of a Cabbage Patch Kid, another unusual first in a seemingly endless string of them. Xavier would have loved the event, which was chronicled in the *Fort Worth Star-Telegram:* "Clutching a pigtailed doll as she sat in District Judge Robert L. Wright's lap, a 9-year-old Bedford girl became an adoptive parent and an adopted daughter on Valentine's Day.

"Leslie Ann Golden legally adopted her Cabbage Patch doll look-alike, Cassandra Lynn, which she received as a Christmas gift. During the same ceremony, Leslie was adopted by her stepfather, Dennis Golden.

" 'It has been well-known that since Dec. 25, 1983, this doll, of Cabbage Patch heritage, has been loved, cuddled, snuggled, hugged, held, admired, and, for all intents and purposes, has been the recipient of Leslie Ann Golden's complete and total affection,' Wright's decree read."

A Canadian psychology professor, Hildy Ross of the University of Waterloo, talked about "the chance of misleading the child about adoption." Professor Ross, who specializes in early childhood development, believes that scientific methods are preferable when explaining the birth process. "I personally favor that approach," she said, "to an approach that promotes additional legends or misconceptions. You can deal just as nicely with the truth."

Xavier stayed with the adoption concept not because it was socially desirable but because the idea worked. Well-meaning critics told him time and again that sales people would not go through the rigamarole, to which his reply was, "then they can't be part of an adoption center."

"It was just a matter of educating them," Xavier says, though surely more was involved than that, "and getting them excited. The whole key is to generate enthusiasm about our marketing concepts, so it's very important that we work with the shop owner. I don't believe any product or idea can be marketed successfully unless it's taken from the drawing board with a great deal of enthusiasm. In our case, we've got to sell the shop owners on the entire concept, from the birth certificates right on down to the special words we use — and don't use.

"For instance, we correct them in a nice way if they use the word 'doll,' by saying, 'Oh, don't call him that, you'll hurt his feelings. He's a *baby*.' When they say 'buy,' we'll say 'adopt.' Before very long they're using those terms too. Then we'll talk about a certain bald baby having diaper rash, or mention how another curly-headed blond is fond of animals, and how another with freckles has been so naughty he has to be set in the corner. Before you know it, they start to talk about them the same way."

On March 6, 1984, Bernard and Joan McNamara appeared on the *Today Show* with Betty Furness to discuss the Cabbage Patch Kids, and specifically the adoption issue. Their appearance generated an avalanche of mail, pro and con, and was one of the most thought-provoking discussions of the subject in the media.

Bernard McNamara is executive director of the Family Resources Adoption Program, an Ossining, New York, agency specializing in finding homes for hard-to-place youngsters. Joan McNamara, Bernard's wife and the author of several major books on the subject, is an "adoption specialist" with the same agency.

The McNamaras are a couple that could rightly be called heroic. They have twelve children of their own, *ten of them adopted*. And the jobs they hold are among the most difficult in the entire field of adoption: the children they attempt to place are "emotionally handicapped," often to a severe extent, and have problems of one sort or another that make most prospective parents shy away. They are not cute white babies with long lists of affluent, childless couples clamoring to adopt them. Some of the children come from terrible, nightmarish backgrounds; others are of an older age that somehow makes them "undesirable."

The remarkable McNamaras know firsthand of what they talk, and their enthusiasm is high for the adoption concept of the Cabbage Patch Kids. "For once," states Bernard McNamara, "someone is finally saying that adopted kids are wanted."

This is important, as everyone in the adoption field can agree, since the children themselves often feel alone, almost like lepers, as if somehow being without parents is their fault. Even better, if the children are not winsome or otherwise physically attractive, not modeling agency examples of what children are "supposed" to look like, the fuss made over the adopted Cabbage Patch Kids builds the idea that all youngsters are valuable.

Bernard McNamara says "even hardened, tough teens react positively" to the adoption message the Cabbage Patch Kids convey.

The McNamaras have found that mothers who adopted out their own children were negative about the marketing concept developed by Xavier, while adults who as children had been adopted were largely in favor of it. The McNamaras themselves entertain no doubts about the value of the Cabbage Patch Kids.

Bernard and Joan McNamara provide preparation courses for both children and their prospective parents, and have found the Cabbage Patch Kids to be valuable tools in explaining the adoption process. Especially important is the message that the dolls, adopted just as the children are about to be, are greatly loved and cherished.

Bernard McNamara tells the story of how a Cabbage Patch Kid helped with a seven-year-old boy he himself adopted. The boy, despite his age, had previously had responsibility for his four younger brothers and sisters, a not uncommon occurrence for children with youthful mothers who do not know how to cope with the stresses of raising a family.

The seven-year-old boy was a quiet sort — passive — a youngster who never seemed to cause disturbances or trouble. But clearly something was bothering him. Bernard McNamara handed a Cabbage Patch Kid to the child, watched him cuddle and hug the doll. "Then it was like a dam breaking loose," McNamara recalls.

The Cabbage Patch Kid had reminded the child of his baby brother, about how much he missed the baby for whom he had cared. The seven-year-old talked about his brother, and soon was opening up about everything that bothered him, and of course there was plenty. Worries that had festered in his mind were brought forward for discussion, and once revealed they could be dealt with lovingly, with concern and compassion.

"Children can relate to the Cabbage Patch Kids," says Bernard McNamara with conviction. "I have no doubt of it. For the first time many of the children are viewing adoption in a positive light. They see that people care for and really love these dolls."

The explosive adoption issue Xavier stirred up, ultra-sensitive because of the naked, deep-felt emotions involved, likely will remain controversial for as long as the Cabbage Patch Kids are popular. But it is hard to see anything evil in the practice when you listen to Bernard and Joan McNamara, who live with the problem from two sides: that of adoptive parents, and as concerned, expert professionals trying to find loving environments for homeless children.

• 10 •

Coleco Comes to the Cabbage Patch

Three new editions of dolls were introduced in January, 1982. The first to appear were the New 'Ears Preemies, 5,000 of them, the first Preemies to be born with ears. Right on the heels of the New 'Ears Preemies (there had been 15,000 New 'Ears babies in the edition the year before) came the 1982 Unsigned Edition, 15,000 in all. Again, this represented a substantial drop in production, the 1980/1981 Unsigned Edition numbering, ultimately, 73,650. Nevertheless, if 1982 were to be a year of cutting back, it would also be the time when the groundwork would be laid for the incredible successes of 1983, and the utterly spectacular developments of 1984.

Also introduced in 1982 were 10,000 Little People Pals, retail cost $75, which were dolls for dolls. The Little People, of course, being people (or at least a "special race" discovered by Xavier in the cabbage patch) needed something to play with, just as their "parents" did. These Little People Pals were signed by Xavier, and came with a certificate of authenticity.

By now Xavier had branched into a variety of related products, though nowhere near the bewildering amount that would be offered later. There was a Stork Poster, $3; a Marilyn Suzanne necklace, the portrait of a Cabbage Patch Kid on a medallion, set against an ivory or black background, $5; a "Professional Collection" of clothes, meaning the choice of a doctor's uniform, nurse's uniform, candy striper, or scrub suit, $15; "Message" tee-shirts — "Have you HUGGED your Little People Baby?" or "I came Special Delivery from the Cabbage Patch," for example — in various colors, $5; a Xavier Roberts tee-shirt, Xavier's portrait on the front, $10; and Debonair Xavier Bear, a soft-sculpture animal, $75.

Debonair Xavier Bear, who was a cute little fellow, was billed by Original Appalachian Artworks as the successor to the teddy bear. "But let's face it. The 'Teddy' bear was a product of an earlier era, a time before the airplane and automobile were commonplace; a time before microwave ovens and cable TV; a time — though it may be hard to believe — even before digital watches!

"Yes, the 'Teddy' bear has grown old. Roosevelt isn't president any more, and even if he was, he would be 124 years old. Imagine how your friends would react if you told them you had a bear named after a 124-year-old president.

"No, the sad but true fact of the matter is that old 'Teddy' is simply out of step with these changing times. After all, how can you talk about the Space Shuttle or computer graphics with a bear who still thinks the wireless telegraph is a big deal?

"But what, you ask, is a bear lover such as yourself to do?

"Not to worry. Because now there is a new bear for the 1980s. Not only is he 'hip,' 'with it,' 'far out' and 'funky,' but he also has impeccable manners, and is just as suave and debonair as you please.

"Did I say 'debonair?' If so, then it should not surprise you to learn that the name of this cool customer just happens to be — you guessed it! — Debonair Bear."

No matter how successful Debonair Xavier Bear became through the efforts of Original Appalachian Artworks, the fact is that the company could only do so much. Xavier recognized this and looked for the right "tie-in" with a major company that could open up for his babies the unlimited markets he knew they deserved. The enterprising Paula Osborne, one of the original five who formed the company on little more than hope and prayers, was also very involved in the search for a deep pocket.

Two years older than Xavier, Paula had known the young artist for several years before going into business with him. They had met originally through Paula's sister, Cindy, who attended White County High School with Xavier. But the future president, Paula, and chairman of the board, Xavier, became really close friends while Paula worked as a waitress at Unicoi State Park. Xavier managed the state-owned craft shop, and, of course, was busily adopting out his Little People, both at Unicoi and at area art shows.

The ambitious Georgia artist, still in college, invited Paula Osborne to help him make his artwork, because the demand was more than he could handle on his own. Xavier trained Paula on how to stitch the babies while she continued as a waitress at Unicoi. The waitress, in less than a decade, became president of a company whose dolls and related products would have annual sales of more than $1 *billion.*

In the early days of the company, Paula worked in every aspect of production, but was especially valuable training others. When the young Georgians began traveling to national gift shows, Paula was along in her role as a nurse. Like Xavier, she possessed boundless energy.

Paula became, first, a vice president in charge of production, and in the summer of 1982, president of the company. She had long agreed with Xavier that the direction for growth of the babies was in the field of licensing, and steadily pursued the goal. Not long after she became president of Original Appalachian Artworks, she contracted the services of Schlaifer Nance & Company as exclusive licensing agents for the Cabbage Patch Kids. And not long after that, the deal which was to make Xavier enormously rich was struck with Coleco.

Before that occurred, however, there was an appearance on ABC-TV's "You Asked For It," hosted by Rich Little, which proved again (if it ever needed proving) that getting publicity for the Little People was no problem. Getting the product distributed to the masses was.

Xavier was also busy in the Spring of 1982 considering plans for Fantasy World, an amusement park he envisioned rivaling the finest Disney had been able to create. "It will be a place," Xavier says, "where people can come and just get lost in the fantasy . . . maybe with the tourists wearing costumes instead of the performers. We'll set up video cameras everywhere, so people can perform and watch each other on television." Fantasy World is not yet a reality, but may become one. Xavier has purchased 430 acres of land just north of Cleveland, Georgia, in magnificent mountain country, a site which for natural beauty is hands-down superior to rival amusement parks. And while the money wasn't available to proceed in 1982, every indication is it will be in the near future.

The World's Fair was held in Knoxville, Tennessee, in 1982, and not surprisingly, perhaps, one of the most popular stopping-in places was not part of the fair itself, but a Babyland General Clinic located just two blocks away. The clinic provided a Little People babysitting service for parents who didn't want to carry their dolls around the fairgrounds, and provided a tour for visitors. They could watch an "actual delivery" taking place, witness a Little Person being operated upon in surgery, and hear the Babyland Singers sing. Little Persons were adopted out to country singer Jeannie C. Riley, the Alabama band, and television host Bryant Gumbel.

One thing that didn't change about Xavier was the energy, thought, and determination he had given to all of his early work. If anything, these increased when he was threatened by an economy over which he had no control. Having tasted a measure of success, and liking it, made the possibility of it slipping from his reaches all the more painful. Xavier preached again and again that "the babies will die if they're just left to sit on a shelf. It's up to the shop owner to put life in them. If they don't, it won't work, and that's no good for anyone. Uniformity is just as important in our business as it is in a McDonald's Franchise."

McDonald's was selling hamburgers, however, while Xavier was adopting out expensive babies. But what the young artist was saying was that what he had created at Babyland General Hospital was a proven winner, and that these practices should be emulated at adoption centers around the country. "If the baby just sits there and looks like a doll," he said "then all the fantasy we've tried so hard to create is lost. A lifelike setting is the key. The babies should look like they're alive, and that what they are doing is something real babies would do."

There were strong indications in 1982, if only adequate distribution could be arranged, that not only the babies, but related products as well, could be marketed successfully. The book "Xavier Roberts presents Little People Pals" sold 100,000 copies in just two months.

On August 15, 1982, Cleveland, Georgia, was again put on

the map when the *Today Show* and host Betty Furness rolled into town to give early morning NBC viewers a look at Babyland General Hospital. She called Xavier's concept "extremely interesting" and professed "admiration" for everyone connected with it. "I played with dolls when I was young," said Betty Furness, "and I can't understand why my own girls didn't. I do think it's very healthy, though, and I'm glad to see a return to that type of make-believe."

Bryant Gumbel called the Little People Phenomenon "harmless," (this of course before the 1983 Christmas Madness) which brought a remark from a Little Person, "That Bryant Gumbel is so-o-o-o cute. And I think he is harmless, too."

Betty Furness adopted three Little People of her own for her granddaughters, ages 13, 14, and 15. Neither she nor Bryant Gumbel could have known that twenty months hence NBC would be reporting the sacking of stores and the terrorizing of store owners as shoppers battled it out for the in-short-supply dolls.

Not a month went by in 1982 that something didn't occur which kept Babyland General Hospital and the Little People in the news. In April it was the introduction of the Xavier Roberts Designer Clothing Collection, which included a complete selection of casual and dress wear for Little People. Indeed, it was an easy matter, if someone so desired, to spend more money on clothes for a Little Person than on a real child.

In May, 1982, was the announcement of Xavier's becoming chairman of the board of Original Appalachian Artworks, and Paula Osborne being made president of Babyland General. It was made clear that in Xavier's case he shared his position with Otis Lee.

June, 1982, witnessed the introduction of the *Cabbage Patch Dispatch*, a quarterly magazine that soon (at an $8 annual subscription price) would have a circulation of more than 100,000.

In July two more crafts books appeared, *Debonair Xavier Bear* and *Rissa the Ballerina*, and more — a lot more — were in the planning stage. It seemed that almost any conceivable product could be made to have a tie-in with the Little People.

But the big news came in August, the biggest news of all. It would forever change the life of Xavier and his Original Appalachian Artworks. "We're very excited about the agreement and about working with Coleco," said Paula Osborne, announcing that the licensing agreement had been signed. She said the affiliation with Coleco would "increase awareness of the Little People throughout the United States and the world."

The world. The two words came easily from Paula Osborne's lips. Like Xavier and Eula, she was thinking big. The odds had been astronomically long that she and her friends would even have survived six months, much less be signing deals with an industry powerhouse such as Coleco. Interestingly, the big manufacturer wasn't talking about the "world," at least not publicly.

Unbounded optimism prevailed at Babyland. Xavier knew the Coleco deal was what he'd been waiting for, working for, what would indeed vault him to *primus inter pares* among the great doll makers. If he had ever experienced a doubt, he would not admit to it. No amount of success, however great, would surprise him. Or at least so he maintained. In unguarded moments, however, his fear of that deep recession was evident in his words, "It almost got us," and "We came close to not making it."

Xavier would be paid for every doll Coleco produced, for every related item the company would put out, and the amounts involved seemed limitless to the young dreamer. His positive feelings were reflected by pie-in-the-sky publicity releases dispatched from Babyland.

Collectors will be interested to note that this new step for the Little People — combined with their official name change to the Cabbage Patch Kids — will make the earlier editions even more valuable than ever!

In addition, Little People parents will want to collect each new Cabbage Patch Kid accessory as it comes out!

The long and short of it is that the Little People/Cabbage Patch Kids are going to be the hottest things since buttered popcorn.

Yet which one, Coleco or Xavier, actually was the more realistic? "Hotter than buttered popcorn," Xavier said his babies would become, and no one during the 1983 Christmas Madness would disagree. People didn't fight over popcorn, stand in lines in freezing weather for hours to get it. The ink was hardly dry on the contract before the young Georgians were predicting a conclusive success.

After predicting far in advance the marketing success the newly named Cabbage Patch Kids would have, the *Cabbage Patch Dispatch* asked, "But will it change them? Will making the Big Time cause them to get the Big Head?"

"No, definitely not," says Otis Lee, emphatically responding to the question. "We're still our same lovable selves. No amount of success can ever change that. By the way," he adds, "would you like my autograph?" And so, the Cabbage Patch Kids — and everyone associated with them — are ready to move into a new and exciting era, a fun future filled with fabulous flights of fantasy! Well, you get the idea.

Of course, some of the more inventive Kids have already thought of possible video games that could be based on the Babyland characters. Such as *Cabbage Patch Duel*. Or *Stork Wars.*

In the wake of this momentous announcement, a few observations can be made right off. First, the Cabbage Patch Kids — the Little People from Babyland — are destined to become a household word the world over. They are already the darlings of the art and collecting world, and when Coleco kicks off a major advertising program to promote them nationally . . . well, you get the picture . . .

Is it exciting? You bet. Is it great fun? Yep. And who can be more excited and proud than the 200,000 Little People — and their parents — who have watched Babyland grow from an obscure spot tucked away in the mountains of north Georgia in 1978 to the internationally-known point of interest it has become.

But perhaps the sum total of this new giant step for Cab-
bagekind can best be summed up in this candid, unbiased
statement by Billy Badd, who was overheard talking to his
sister, Bobby Jo, about the possibilities.

"I only hope that, if we get to star in a prime time
animated cartoon special, they don't put it on past our
bedtime."

The prime-time animated cartoon special *was* in the future,
as was seemingly everything else Xavier could dream up to
put in the minds of his Cabbage Patch Kids. No longer The Little People, they now became Cabbage Patch Kids. Xavier
would continue to put out his own, more-expensive versions
of the dolls, but under the new name.

"A household word the world over." Even if a manufacturer
really believed such a claim, it likely wouldn't make it about
its product for fear of becoming a laughingstock in the trade.
No such fear existed for Xavier. He'd known it would happen
before he was even in business for himself. By early 1984, the
Cabbage Patch Kids were either selling in, or negotiations
were underway for distribution to, *almost every non-communist
nation in the world*. The dolls, as Xavier had believed, really did
speak an international language. The problem, now to be overcome, was not being without a wide enough market for the
babies. Rather, it was how to produce them fast enough.

Long before the 1983 Madness, a Babyland General Hospital
promotion piece read: "Indications right now are that the Cabbage Patch Kids could very well be the kind of popular and
cultural phenomenon that comes along only once every
decade or so."

It was necessary to assure purchasers of past Little People
that the flooding of the market with mass-produced Cabbage
Patch Kids would not affect the value of their babies. Xavier
wanted to continue to sell his own more-expensive, better-
quality doll, and an important move was to convince that hard
core of buyers who had long supported him that their
previous investments were not only still strong but would be
helped by the introduction of the Cabbage Patch Kids. Xavier
addressed the issue head-on.

"But the question now is this: What does it all mean to Little People parents and collectors?

"Only that your original Little People babies — as well as the new Cabbage Patch Kids limited editions — are going to become even more valuable and collectible than ever! Since there will be *no more* Little People babies delivered from the Cabbage Patch ever again, the babies you have now will become rare collectibles as the years go by, particularly the hand-signed editions. They are particularly attractive to serious collectors because no two are *exactly* alike. Each is an individual work of soft sculpture art, hand stitched to birth by loving doctors and nurses in Cleveland.

"In short, the Little People embody a kind of quality that is becoming harder and harder to find in today's mass-produced world."

"Of course, the new Cabbage Patch Kids editions continue this same tradition of quality, and that's why *they* will become increasingly valuable as time goes by, along with the fact that the 1983 Kids will be available *only* in a series of special limited editions.

"But the facts already bear out that some of the earliest edition Little People have been re-adopted for as much as sixty times their original Adoption fee! Without a doubt, these Kids not only bring the light of love and affection into your home, but, rather than costing money to raise — as most ordinary children do — these can actually *make* money for you!

"Is it any wonder, then, that the nation's latest baby boom is centered right here in the scenic mountains of north Georgia?"

It was probably true that collectors of Xavier's earliest dolls would over the years see a further appreciation in their value. Compared to the number on the market, they were exceedingly scarce. Whether the same would occur with the Cabbage Patch Kids Xavier himself intended to produce, was a different question. They might indeed skyrocket in value, being an elite part of a famous, much-larger group. But perhaps not. The value of a doll to a great extent depends on what people *think* it is worth or, even more basically, what they are willing to pay. Perhaps Coleco's first Cabbage Patch Kids will be the ones bringing the high prices. One need only recall the $3 to $1,000 appreciation of the first Barbies to know that a mass-produced item can also be a collectible.

The licensing agreement with Coleco came along at the right time. Soon the nation would be on its feet again, and like an individual awakening from a long slumber, eager to catch up on what had been missed. Also, in 1982, Original Appalachian Artworks had produced only about 30,000 babies. In 1981 the number had been more than 100,000.

Soon the Cabbage Patch Kids licensing program embraced a sizable list of prestigious companies: Milton Bradley; Colorforms; Wundies; Elkay Industries; Parker Brothers; Riegel Textile; and King-Seely Thermos. But this was just the iceberg's tip. By 1984, cashing in on the Cabbage Patch craze, Xavier would be involved with some seventy manufacturers, who spun off an incredible 250 related products.

And no wonder. It has to be worth money for, say, a food manufacturer to be able to say the Cabbage Patch Kids preferred its brand of cereal. Or a fast-food chain to boast that the Cabbage Patch Kids ate there. Go anywhere in public — a zoo, a theater, a ball game, a restaurant — and there were little children, and sometimes their parents, clutching their babies. Fathers joined with mothers to perpetuate the fantasy that the cuddly doll was indeed a full-fledged member of the family.

The last Little People produced by Xavier were the 1982 Christmas Edition, numbering one thousand and selling for $200 each. These were stamped with Xavier's signature, and autographed as well, and since they were the last to bear the name Little People, were expected to increase rapidly in value. To date they are estimated to be worth $250, though their worth may indeed increase when it sinks in deeply that no more of the dolls that were the foundation of the Cabbage Patch Madness will bear the same name. Males in the edition were called Baby Ruby; females, Christy Nicole. The news of the deal with Coleco was public, and the babies were quickly adopted out.

Schlaifer Nance and Paula Osborne played big roles in consummating the licensing agreement with Coleco, and would continue in the future to ensure that a steady stream of related products would be available to a captivated public. Xavier himself, previously a kind of head cheerleader and nonpareil salesman, would increasingly be cast as an executive. He had trained the others — particularly competent women of whom

Paula Osborne was simply the most obvious example — and had always been skilled at delegating authority wisely. And now everything didn't rest on his shoulders. It was Xavier's genius, hard work, enthusiasm, and vision which had delivered the coup. Although he still had important contributions to make, what would turn out to be the Cabbage Patch Phenomenon could probably, after the licensing agreement with Coleco, have occurred without him. Later, there was even the hint that he recognized the fact that the business was now moving on its own accord; that he could lay back a bit.

"What would you like to do, now that you're rich?" Xavier was asked as the car in which he was riding sped from Atlanta towards Cleveland. It was a bright clear north Georgia day in the spring of 1984, and he was dressed in tennis shoes, old jeans, and Western shirt.

"I'm going to make a lot more money. I've got plenty of plans on where the money can be used."

"The amusement park?"

"I don't know. Some times things you plan on don't work out."

"Money is more important to you than to others?"

"I think it's a measure of success. I wanted to be successful."

"But you've got more time now than before. What are you going to do with it?"

"I'm still very busy. Always traveling. I've learned a lot about geography, I can tell you that."

"But the pace has to have slowed."

"I wouldn't say that. But I do *take* time for things I like to do. I like to build things. Work with my hands. Pottery and sculpture. I enjoy planting things and watching them grow."

"You're a talented artist. I assume you are. Do you think being so commercial so early helped develop your ability?"

"Maybe not."

"All that time building the company was time away from your art."

"The two weren't exclusive. What I did required a lot of creativity."

"Was the money more important than the art?"

"I've thought about it. Do you know what I'd really like to do now? I'd like to go back to school and study art."

"Seems like you could be *teaching* art, not studying it."

"There's a lot I don't know. I didn't continue with it long enough, quitting to start the business, and all. I really need to learn more. It would be good. Go back to school and pick up where I left off."

Certainly Xavier could afford any school he chose.

Soon after the licensing agreement was reached with Coleco, there was talk of an animated cartoon series done in collaboration with Hanna-Barbera. This has since been put on hold, replaced with a prime-time special scheduled for Christmas 1984, with other specials on the drawing board.

Towards the end of 1982, the big excitement at Babyland General Hospital was anticipating the Coleco program, which everyone seemed convinced would make the babies known worldwide. Still, during the waiting, there were events that would have been highlights in the histories of most companies. For example, former British Prime Minister Harold Wilson came to north Georgia to speak at a college, and the school's president asked Xavier if he would have Sir Harold picked up in his limousine. Xavier did more. He presented the surprised Wilson with a Little Person, and watched solemnly as the powerful former prime minister signed the adoption papers.

Ten Cabbage Patch Kids began regularly to be featured in the *Cabbage Patch Dispatch,* and these clearly were the characters from which Xavier hoped the producers of his prime-time animated special would find their "stars." Just as a "Peanuts" special wouldn't seem complete without Charley Brown, Snoopy, Lucy, Linus, Schroeder, and Peppermint Patti, Xavier believed *individual* Cabbage Patchers, not just the generic whole, should start to achieve fame. The Terrific Ten were described as follows:

There is *Otis L.,* a bald boy named after Otis Lee, the leader of the gang. Though he often finds himself in more trouble than he bargained for, you can bet that Otis has a plan up his sleeve, and that he'll manage to get out of it somehow.

And meet *Sybil S.,* a blonde girl with pigtails whose enthusiasm sometimes gets her into a fix or two of her own. If she weren't so sweet-natured, some of the other Kids might call her a show-off. As it is, they simply smile and say, "She's just being Sybil."

Tyler B., on the other hand, is a little black boy with curls who just loves to show off, and does so every chance he gets. In fact, many of his friends call him by his nickname: "Showboat." Naturally, he loves all the attention.

And don't forget *Marilyn S.*, the champagne ponytailed fashionplate of the group. She's already made a splash in the world of style with her very own designer jewelry.

And you'll love the antics of *Billy B.* and his sister, *Bobbie J.*, twins who go everywhere and do everything together. Their personalities perfectly match their flaming red hair and freckles.

Rebecca R. is as cute as she can be with her champagne ponytails, even if she is shy and does tend to s-s-stutter a bit. *Gilda R.*, though, with her gold braids and winning ways, is the life of the party. You'll want to get to know them both.

Amy L. would rather play tennis than probably just about anything else. "She really has quite a racket," says Otis of her, and when you see her beautiful auburn pigtails and flashing smile, you'll know just what he means.

Last — but certainly not least — is plain *Dorothy J.*, although with her pretty brown curls, she is really anything but "plain." Just give her a little love and attention, and you've made a friend for life.

Sales were down in 1982 over the previous year, but Xavier's popularity was not. Remarkable letters poured into Babyland General Hospital, mostly from children but not a few from adults, singing his praises in a manner even his own hardly reticent public relations people might have blushed at. And the Kids took their bows as well.

From Charity Worley, Conyers, Georgia:

> I have five babies, but all of them have problems. Terrie Samantha is very shy. Darlene Lannette has a very bad illness only a special medicine called "Dimton Slide B" can cure. I have no money to buy it with. Tiffanie Nicole is so small and can't understand she can't mess the house up, and if she keeps up the house will be falling down! Scott Richard is the only boy, and he feels so lonely. And Belinda Sassy is so scared about living here, she hasn't come yet.

From Becky Euell, Jerseyville, Illinois:

> I got Sydney Wilda March 5, 1983. When I took her home, all my friends said, "All it is is a stupid doll that your dad bought ya." But they don't know that she can change channels and turn the TV on and off.

From Michelle Boone, Ladson, South Carolina:

> I adopted a little girl named Gilda Trudy, and she means the world to me! But sometimes she says she sees monsters in her bed, so then I put her in bed with me.

And it wasn't just letters. Shara Stoddard, age 10, won a *Weekly Reader* essay contest for a piece entitled "My Hero."

> Xavier Roberts is my hero. His artistic skill and hard work created the "Little People" which are sold all over the world.

> I admire Xavier Roberts very much because he succeeded by his own efforts and because he made my own dear Neil Adora.

Shara was right. Xavier did succeed because of his own efforts, though the five who started out with him also deserve a share of the praise. They set up, against all odds, an extraordinarily successful business. But making the concept a profit-generating machine such as the industry has perhaps never before witnessed was a company with its own remarkable past and present.

The Connecticut Leather Company

The company to which Xavier tied his star, Coleco, was founded in 1932 during the Great Depression by a young immigrant named Maurice Greenberg. It would become known as the Connecticut Leather Company (Connecticut incorporation, 1961), Coleco for short. At the outset, the company was viable, partly because Maurice Greenberg (Xavier's kindred spirit where hard work was concerned) was willing to put in long hours of intelligent labor, and partly because, even during the depths of the Depression, people needed to have their shoes repaired. Maurice Greenberg provided leather to shoe repairers.

Leonard Greenberg, currently chief executive officer of Coleco, Maurice's son, joined the company at a young age in the 1940s, and persuaded his father to branch into the leather-craft business. In the 1950s came further expansion into plastic army helmets and toys for children, plastic toboggans, snow coasters and, finally, a backyard wading pool. By the 1960s, Coleco had established itself as a major toy and pool company, and the success continued into the next decade.

In 1976, Coleco became the first major toy company to enter the electronic games arena with the introduction of its "Telstar" video game. Through ColecoVision and popular video games such as "Donkey Kong," "Lady Bug," and "Q-Bert," the company was an unquestioned leader in the home video revolution. In short, Coleco had the kind of proven track record for which Xavier had been searching. The company designed, manufactured, and marketed some *one thousand products,* including different models and variations of the same item. There were family leisure games, video games, pool tables, doll carriages, plastic ride-on vehicles, air action hockey games, home pinball machines, plastic snow products, sports action games, table top games, wading pools, swimming pools, pool accessories, sandboxes, and a broad variety of other products.

The Cabbage Patch Kids would turn out to be the hottest selling item Coleco ever handled. Incredibly, Mattel, in what might be considered one of the worst decisions ever made by a toy company, turned down the chance to market the Kids, as did several other companies. For Coleco, as will be seen, they were a godsend.

The actual making of the deal with Coleco was fraught with irony. Some people at Coleco weren't that enthusiastic when licensing agent Roger Schlaifer approached them through a direct mailing in March, 1982. But Coleco senior vice president Al Kahn did visit Schlaifer (who was responsible for naming the dolls Cabbage Patch Kids) in June, 1982, in Atlanta, and Kahn more than anyone was captivated by the idea. "But it was a tough sell," Roger Schlaifer says, recalling that many people at Coleco remained unconvinced. The irony was that, in any way of reasoning, it was Xavier who was offering Coleco the good deal.

Under instructions from Xavier, Roger Schlaifer insisted that the concepts behind the kids — birth certificates, adoption papers, references to their being babies, etc. — needed to be retained, and there were those at Coleco, of course, who did not believe they needed to be guided by the opinions of an upstate rural Georgian. This was the mighty manufacturer of "Telstar" and "Donkey Kong," a powerhouse in the toy industry. Coleco was certain it could prosper without Xavier; how he would do without them was another question.

Mattel had turned the idea down, as had Fisher-Price, Ideal, and Tamy. (How they feel now is a different matter.) But Al Kahn was enthusiastic, (it was he who wanted to retain the one-of-a-kind concept for the Kids), and his opinions carried the day at Coleco. Less than two months after the visit in Atlanta, the deal was cut.

Xavier received no advance payment from Coleco, which

was unusual for him. Almost always, if his products are to be used, a cash payment (plus royalties) is required. Instead Coleco promised to "spend millions" (Roger Schlaifer won't say how many) advertising the dolls, and to assign its "best people" to the project. Xavier would receive a royalty from every doll sold anywhere (no one will say how much), and had final control over quality. If he didn't approve, the product didn't reach the market place.

Coleco left nothing to chance. The dolls simply weren't deposited on a store shelf with hopes they would sell. Ruth Manko, a psychologist, market researcher, and president of R.M. Manko Associates in Montclair, New Jersey, was retained by Coleco and began to study the product just a month after the licensing agreement had been signed. "We asked," said Mrs. Manko, "women, parents of children ten and under, to our first Cabbage Patch Kid group sessions in Chicago." From a mirror in an observation room, Coleco officials watched closely. The women, Mrs. Manko said, "held the dolls on their laps, stroked them, held their hands, took off their sweaters when they thought it had become too warm. One woman I remember was knitting a sweater for her doll." At this initial session the women were encouraged to discuss their feelings of birth and adoption.

"These observation sessions," wrote Fred Ferretti for *The New York Times*, "held with the permission of the women involved, were quiet introductions to the dolls. Mrs. Manko . . . and her research team and the manufacturers saw and defined at these sessions the feeling that grew into a national buying craze."

Other sessions were held in New Jersey suburbs, Chicago, and Atlanta. There were numerous individual interviews, as psychologists probed for people's feelings. Adoptive parents were contacted. Coleco commissioned psychological studies to be made by some of the genuine heavyweights in the field. The company, in fact, could predict in advance that it had a winner, a big one, yet it came up short where production was concerned.

None of this surprised Xavier. Expensive psychological studies merely confirmed for him what he'd already seen, that his dolls possessed an indefinable but very real appeal. What the studies did accomplish was to pinpoint those qualities of the dolls which could be exploited to the maximum.

The Cabbage Patch Kids, said Ruth Manko, are popular not only because they "could be held and felt, but they were not beautiful, and we know that babies are not always so beautiful."

"Equally important," Fred Ferretti wrote, "was the concept of uniqueness. Using computers to keep track of its dolls, the company, despite having almost 3 million of the dolls produced in Hong Kong, says it has managed to keep each one individual by changing characteristics such as eye color, freckles, hair, dimples and clothing."

"Each doll," said Ruth Manko, "is different, so it became true that nobody has a doll like yours. The process was me, mine, my doll, my baby. And it could be 'adopted' legally, with papers to show for it."

The Cabbage Patch Kids produced by Coleco were made with a vinyl face, while the more expensive version put out by Xavier has fabric faces. Coleco advertised the dolls with a heavy television campaign — most on Saturday mornings — first introducing the Kids in June, 1983, in New York. The dolls sold out instantly. Coleco, after awhile, simply suspended advertising. "We don't need to spend the money," said Barbara Wruck, the company's director of corporate communications.

"Things happened on their own momentum," said public relations director Robert Wiener. "Originally, of course, it wasn't that way."

In marketing circles the selling of the Cabbage Patch Kids was considered a *tour de force*, even Xavier was generally pleased, but others, like Dr. Charles W. Faulkner, writing in the *St. Louis American*, were less than enthusiastic.

> Why did children find out about the dolls before their parents? Why were parents the last to know? The answer lies in advertising. The answer can be found in your television set on Saturday morning. The reason is a carefully orchestrated advertising campaign directed at your sweet little kids. So, Saturday morning while you

were sleeping late or chit-chatting on the phone with your next door neighbor, your sweet little child was being scientifically brainwashed by those powerful commercials that appear on those harmless children's cartoon shows.

Brainwash the child and the child will brainwash the parent. That is exactly what happened. Psychologists who help prepare television commercials decided that they would make Christmas 1983 the year of the doll. Next year it might be the year of the jumping rope. This year, the key to the gold mine for toy makers is the Cabbage Patch doll. But parents would never buy such an ugly little doll for their kids — unless the children absolutely demanded it. This is how the shrewd advertisers reasoned: "We'll have millions of lovely little kids writing Santa asking for our Cabbage Patch dolls. No parent in his right mind would want a child to lose faith in Santa and be emotionally disabled for all of 1984. So, let's aim our commercials at those emotionally defenseless, impressionable, manipulative kids. We can make them want anything. They will make their parents buy the dolls. Then, when parents realize how desperate their children are for the dolls we will publicize the fact that the dolls are in short supply. Let's show some scenes of eager parents breaking down doors of stores to get the dolls. Let's get parents excited by showing pictures of disappointed parents unable to get the dolls and fearful of breaking their sweet child's heart. This will make the dolls status symbols and drive parents into a Cabbage Patch doll buying frenzy."

The ads and the television commercials were clever pieces of work, but no one at Coleco could have predicted that Jane Pauley would feature the Kids on the Today Show, that Nancy Reagan would give two of them away to visiting children from South Korea, that Johnny Carson couldn't seem to mention them often enough on his program, or that Bob Hope would feature them on a national TV special. Nor could the headline-grabbing riots have been foreseen. "Less than five hundred thousand dollars" was spent advertising the Cabbage

Patch Kids in 1983, according to Robert Wiener, and less will be spent in 1984, when sales are expected to be *four times* as great.

Everyone, Coleco found, seemed to want a Cabbage Patch Kid. Steven Kolker, Coleco senior vice president, was often told, when he was trying to arrange a business meeting, "Okay, if you bring along a free doll." On the reverse side, when people called Coleco's ad agency to talk to the president, Richard Schwarzchild, they had to assure his secretary that they weren't looking for a free Cabbage Patch Kid.

Robert Wiener says "you have no idea" the gambits people tried to use on Coleco to get free dolls. One television show's producers asked for and received twenty-four of the Kids to be used as "background," but only two were left on the set when the program ended. Coleco executives on the talk show circuit had to carry the dolls around in "brown paper bags," lest they be mobbed by casual passersby.

Coleco, for all the market research it put into the Cabbage Patch Kids, originally considered the dolls as merely a Christmas toy. But the frenzy that greeted the product caused the company to change its mind. "The Cabbage Patch Kids," said The New York Times, "are now a year-round item, and as soon as there is enough product, or when there is a new product, TV advertising will be unleashed again."

How brilliant was Coleco? No one connected with the Cabbage Patch Kids, least of all Xavier, whose fortune increases each time one of the Kids or any one of 250 related products is sold, is complaining about the results. But the company seemed to have missed several beats. It says the shortages were not intentional, and if so (industry analysts have doubts) this by itself indicates that Coleco was not a master Svengali. Also, the company did not seem prepared for the numerous complaints from adoption groups, criticism that probably could have been blunted had it been known that the preponderance of expert opinion was in favor of the concept.

In 1982, before Coleco signed the licensing agreement with Xavier, the Connecticut company was *the* most successful traded on the New York Stock Exchange — its stock rose a phenomenal 434%! This was the year of "Donkey Kong," but even though the Cabbage Patch Kids followed in 1983,

Coleco's fortunes took a downturn. For it was not Xavier's cuddly dolls that the company bet on in 1983, but a computer named Adam, and Coleco's experience with that much ballyhooed high-tech gadget was a disaster. Yet ups and downs were nothing new for Coleco. "A graph of the company's profits and sales over the last 10 years," said the *Los Angeles Times*, "forms a jagged line so sharp you could cut yourself on it."

The line was mostly down in the second half of 1983, despite having the top-selling first-year doll in history. In June, when the Adam home computer was announced for August to favorable reviews, Coleco stock was at 44. In July it was down to 36, as reports surfaced that Adam would not be delivered on time. The stock was at 31 in September (Adam's shipment date was missed), 26 in October (there were "bugs" in the computer), 21 in December (only 140,000 of a proposed 500,000 computers had been shipped). As *Business Week* magazine pointed out, "An astounding 38% of the 10 million shares of Coleco common not held by company executives (and 23% of the total 16.5 million shares outstanding) have been sold short in the anticipation that the stock price will decline below recent levels . . . ."

"Investors are selling the West Hartford (Conn.) toymaker short because they believe that it is having problems in several important areas at once: It is experiencing a shortfall in cash flow, a growing inventory, and difficulties in building volume production of Adam, its new, highly publicized home computer. Even though the company sold every Cabbage Patch doll that it could fly in from Hong Kong this year — about $60 million worth — its cash flow from sales will not be nearly as large as it had expected, primarily because of lower shipments of Adam."

It was almost unbelievable. Coleco had by far the hottest selling item in the hottest selling month of the year, December, yet it was swimming in an ocean of red ink. The company lost $35 million in the fourth quarter of 1983, and sales declined 14% from the previous year.

Barron's, the financial magazine, talked about how popular the Cabbage Patch Kids were at Macy's, then took a hard look at Coleco. "But if you tear yourself away from Macy's Cabbage

Patch and head for the electronics department, you'll find nary an Adam on display, despite all the hoopla — and promises of big Christmas sales — attending its introduction at a trade show last summer. First, the computers were supposed to be shipped in August, then the company moved its deadline to mid-September, and then to mid-October, when some orders actually were shipped. But Macy's, like many another retailer, is still waiting. Mid-December, they're now told, though Coleco concedes its Adam output will be way below its earlier predictions. Meanwhile, down 34th Street at arch-rival Gimbel's, the electronics buyers who had counted themselves fortunate to receive and sell out a few shipments of Adams, are now watching customers return 60% of them, says buyer John Young. Half are griping about the tape drive; the others, the printer, he reports.

"And so it goes in stores throughout the land. The Adam, thus far, has been a marketing nightmare for Coleco; the Cabbage Patch dolls, on the other hand, the stuff of dreams. And the juxtaposition of the two, one very high tech, the other very low — launched within months of each other — brings into sharp relief the fact that Coleco's approach to peddling them has been virtually the same."

It was true. Which led to the inescapable question, if it was not Coleco's genius, its unique methods of marketing and promoting, that made the Cabbage Patch Kids the retail rage of 1983, might it not have been Xavier's overall concept (birth certificates, adoption papers, calling them babies, etc.) and his quality product? Could *anyone* have taken the soft sculpture babies and done as well? The truth is, all the reactions which in sum make up the Cabbage Patch Phenomenon were in evidence before Coleco entered the picture. The Cabbage Patch Kids received national attention only because they were available on a much grander scale than Xavier could provide.

Things change. When the licensing agreement was signed, Xavier probably needed Coleco more than the toy industry giant needed him. Coleco had the distribution, the advertising capital, the wherewithal to get the dolls into the big stores where they would at least have a *chance*. But in 1982 Coleco had to figure it could survive nicely enough without Xavier and the Cabbage Patch Kids. But now the embattled Coleco, looking for some good news to give anxious stockholders, was predicting that it would show a profit by the second quarter of 1984, because of, said the Wall Street Journal, "expected higher sales and profit from its line of Cabbage Patch dolls. The company said it expected revenue from the dolls in all of 1984 to be 'several times as great' as its $60 million in doll revenue last year."

During the 1983 Madness, much of the stitching, stuffing, and dressing of the Cabbage Patch Kids was done in China. The plastic heads, on the other hand, were molded and the yarn-hair implanted in Hong Kong. "The Cabbage Patch Kids," said Kenneth Ting, head of Kader Industrial Co., which is under contract to Coleco to make the babies, "are the ugliest dolls I have ever seen. They're nothing special. I like them because they make me money, but I think American people are crazy."

"A tour," wrote Adi Ignatius of the Wall Street Journal, "through Kader's factory in Hong Kong's North Point district might cause some kids to lose their fascination with the Cabbage Patch Kids. Plastic bags crammed with dozens of naked, headless doll bodies lie waiting to be fitted with noggins. Elsewhere, newly molded heads with vacant eyes are stuck onto metal spokes where machines implant hair onto them. The floor is piled high with boxes of disposable diapers, which are fitted onto each doll before they are clothed. Dozens of young women work quietly, tending to the assembly-line tasks.

"A look around the plant casts doubts on Coleco's assertion that no two dolls are alike. Piles upon piles of dolls are identical in every respect: expression, hairstyle and color, clothing. Says Mr. Ting, 'Well, their names will all be different.' "

Labor costs less in China than in Hong Kong. Women in China making Cabbage Patch Kids were paid about $90 a month, lower than the cost of a week's work in the United States. Hong Kong workers received about $180 a month. But there were problems in China that didn't occur in Hong Kong. The workers would leave their factories during the summer and fall to help bring in the rice harvest.

Coleco sold some six million Cabbage Patch Kids in the nine months ending in March, 1984. Currently the company is producing a *million a month* and cannot keep up with demand. A single toy store in New Jersey has five thousand people on a waiting list for Cabbage Patch Kids, and waiting lists of a thousand or more are common. The dolls are now also manufactured in Mexico, Spain, and Japan. During the 1983 Madness, three 747s were chartered by Coleco to fly the dolls from the Far East to the U.S., and the result was chaos. Greater shortages, says Coleco, are a virtual certainty in 1984.

Edmund K.S. Young, a vice president of Perfekta, another Hong Kong manufacturer of Cabbage Patch Kids under contract with Coleco, said the Cabbage Patch craze was unprecedented in his experience. "The Rubik Cube," said Young, whose company also manufactured that product, "was popular, but no one had to fight for it."

The sweet success of the Cabbage Patch Kids took away some of the sour taste from the Adam fiasco. In January, 1984, said Herbert Kline, president of Markline Inc., an electronics catalog retailer, demand for Adam "took a nose dive." Kline said the drop in demand was caused by a whopping price increase for the computer, the lack of availability of software for the unit, and concerns about Adam's reliability. Worse, JC Penney Company cancelled its remaining orders because the computer failed Penney's own quality tests.

Coleco's big fourth quarter, 1983, profit loss strapped the company for cash, and there was even scattered talk that the company might not survive at all. Always a corporation known for heavy promotion of its products, Coleco had to cut back on advertising because of the cash shortage. It was revealed that Coleco had to cancel some $500,000 in first-quarter ads with NBC.

The situation went from bad to worse. The highly respected *Consumer Reports*, in its January issue, reported that it could not review Adam because it had been unable to buy a working model!

"Coleco bet the company on the Adam," said Milton Berg, a First Investors Corporation portfolio manager, "and even if they work out the bugs, they missed the opportunity this Christmas." *Business Week*, January 9, 1984, reported, "The impact of the delay in shipping Adam already was becoming apparent by the end of the third quarter. Coleco's third-quarter sales amounted to only $114.5 million, 31% behind the same period in 1982. Even worse, third-quarter profits totaled only $2.3 million — just a fraction of the $17.6 million recorded in the third quarter of 1982. Inventories doubled from a year earlier, hitting $161 million as parts for unfinished Adams collected in warehouses. And although the company had plenty of orders for Adam, it had only $107,000 in cash and equivalents, down from $52 million at year-end 1982."

To top everything off, Coleco had to go into urgent negotiations with its lenders, an 11-bank consortium headed by the Rockefeller Chase Manhattan, to extend the payback period on a $196 million revolving line of credit. Fortunately for Coleco, most of these difficulties were overcome, and thanks could largely be attributed to Xavier and his soft-sculpture dolls.

Thus, while Coleco provided Xavier's babies with the wide exposure he believed they deserved, Xavier's product turned out to be an absolute savior for the big Connecticut company. Consider the following startling fact: in 1983, Coleco's sales from *all* products amounted to $596.5 million; in May, 1984, for the Cabbage Patch Kids and related products alone, the company had more than $200 million in unfilled orders, with the amount rising every day.

Two hundred million dollars! These were just unfilled orders; they didn't include goods already delivered and paid for, nor the expected avalanche of requests as the Christmas season draws nearer. The creation of the young mountain man — twenty-eight years old — was now the hub of mighty Coleco's product line.

Nor was lack of advertising money likely to be a problem. The Cabbage Patch Kids really don't need extensive advertising. They are a self-generating promotion mechanism on a scale perhaps never before witnessed in retailing history.

Xavier's product may even force Coleco to change its traditional way of doing business. "The problem at Coleco," said David S. Leibowitz, an analyst with New York-based American Securities Corporation, "is their business is almost entirely dependent on the highly promoted products. They are always on the cutting edge of the latest fad."

But, as the *Los Angeles Times* pointed out, "The toy and game industry, generally speaking, breaks down into two categories:

stable products and highly promoted products. Stable products are those, like Raggedy Ann dolls or Monopoly games, that sell year after year in predictable quantities. Highly promoted products are those, such as E.T. dolls, that generally have a short life span and require heavy advertising, but can score enormous profits."

But the Cabbage Patch Kids show every indication of fitting into *both* categories; stable and fad. The peak has not yet been reached, regardless of those memorable crowd scenes around Christmas, 1983, as evidenced by the huge number of dolls already on order for 1984. But when the mayhem does end, every sign points to the Kids becoming a stable seller, as reliable and bankable as Raggedy Ann or Barbie or Teddy. Working in their favor is their uniqueness, the growing belief they may become collectibles, and the fact that an entire fantasy world — spurred on by prime-time television specials — is still in the process of being created for them, a fantasy world where the cold realities of a troubled planet have no place.

Coleco is also introducing the Koosas, an indefinable species of pets for Cabbage Patch Kids, and Cabbage Patch Kid Pin-Ups, play dolls which come in a realistic setting, such as a store or a filling station. The Pin-Ups are dolls for dolls. In actuality, Coleco is gearing up a mind-numbing variety of Cabbage Patch-related products, including a musical swing, stroller, sleeping bag, and a feeding chair that hooks onto the dining room table so the Cabbage Patch Kid can eat with "his family."

That the Cabbage Patch Kids were becoming *the* major item in Coleco's plans was evidenced by a spate of layoffs at U.S. production facilities. While workers were being hired in Japan, Spain, and Mexico to produce the dolls, workers were being handed pink slips at plants in upstate New York chiefly involved in computer operations. Three hundred employees were laid off in early March; on March 21, there were 118 more; and the axe fell on an additional 1,300 before the month was out.

Meanwhile, Jesmar, the first company to obtain a Cabbage Patch license in Europe, was busily adding employees. The firm intended to manufacture some 10,000 dolls a day, carrying a retail price tag of $25. Only "slight changes" were anticipated for the computerization and programming necessary to achieve the "uniqueness" of which Coleco — and Xavier — were so proud. Of course, Spanish dolls would have Spanish features and names, as would Cabbage Patch Kids for whatever country in which they were sold.

Ten thousand dolls a day in Spain! How many more could be produced in much larger nations — West Germany, England, and Italy, for example — where the standard of living was higher?

As Coleco's Barbara Wruck commented, negotiations are underway or completed in *almost every country in the world*, outside the Communist bloc. Xavier himself, the creator of the Madness (Coleco's address, appropriately, was on Asylum Avenue), saw no reason to believe that any nation would be immune from the appeal of his babies.

• 12 •

Here to Stay? Or Gone Tomorrow?

The Cabbage Patch Phenomenon, called by one critic "thousands of miles wide and an inch deep," may have sunk more sturdy roots than many casual observers initially believed. There were, for example, the thousands of collectors, by nature patient people, not attracted to here-today, gone-tomorrow fads. Their avocational mania for collecting steeled their resolve to dig in for a long haul. Additionally there was a broad mass of millions throughout the country treating the Kids in manners suggesting they would last and become an enduring part of the American landscape. Indeed, much of it was silliness, but silliness associated with home and family, birthdays, weddings, and even death can at times be heart warming, and no one could say with certainty that the Madness would disappear altogether. And the publicity kept streaming in.

Xavier Roberts had forbidden marriages — "The babies are too young" — but one took place in Davenport, Iowa. Edgar Gerard and Jodie Nelly, Cabbage Patch Kids, were bound together in wedlock February 29, 1984, in a service broadcast live over radio station KSTT-AM. "They've been living together for several months," said Norm Grimstead, who had adopted the babies. "We just thought it was about time."

Grimstead gave away the bride and acted as best man, while the ceremony itself was performed by KSTT disc jockey Dave Schropshire. "This may be the first Cabbage Patch wedding," said Schropshire. "I hope it doesn't lead to the first doll divorce."

The first Cabbage Patch marriage, with Edgar Gerard and Jodie Nelly decked out in custom-designed clothes, might have seemed the idea of a rich dilettante, but in reality Grimstead had been out of work for more than a year. "You can't lose your humor because of sad times," he decided.

A week after the Davenport, Iowa, marriage, on March 6, 1984, a Cabbage Patch funeral took place in Corpus Christi, Texas. About fifty small business owners closed their stores during the noon hour for the burial of Baby Rudy. The idea was part of a protest organized by Helen Williams, proprietor of the Second-Hand Rose Antique Store, to demonstrate her displeasure with a manufacturing decision to no longer distribute the Kids through small businesses. A big crowd of merchants were joined by thirty Cabbage Patch Kids, seated as mourners, wearing black armbands and holding flowers, as a record player wailed the lyrics of Willie Nelson's "Georgia on My Mind." Baby Rudy, in a tiny black pine casket, was lowered into a three-foot grave. Earlier, store owners had hung cabbage wreaths on their closed doors and had sent hundreds of dollars worth of flower wreaths to the funeral site.

The *Nation* magazine, normally concerned with serious matters, found in the Cabbage Patch Kids an off-the-wall way to spoof, of all people, the most famous of fundamentalist preachers. "The Reverend Jerry Falwell said that the dolls were blasphemous caricatures. 'According to Holy Scripture,' he said, 'only Adam and Eve had no navels. The hand of atheistic Communism is apparent.'

"Reverend Falwell said that when he first heard of the Cabbage Patch Kids, he had approved of them because 'they taught little girls to think about adoption rather than abortion.' Now, however, he believes they are 'the spawn of Satan.'"

Gerald Thaddeous, Cabbage Patch Kid, was said to be on his way to stardom as an actor. He was described as a "smash hit" in his role as Prince Freddie in a Birmingham, Alabama, Children Theatre's production of "Rumpelstiltskin," and was scheduled to tour with the troupe to Syracuse, Chicago, and Clearwater, Florida.

In Brentwood, Tennessee, Cabbage Patch Kids were formed into a rock and roll group called The Adoption Sisters, and recorded such hits as "Elvira," "Bobbie Sue," and "Fame." In Bellevue, Nebraska, a dress-alike contest was held for Kids and parents, with the object being to become sartorial twins. A Cabbage Patch Kid, Effie May, running on a platform of "sunshine, lollipops, and rainbows," was elected honorary mayor of Palm Harbor, Florida. And in Lanett, Alabama, the hardy Brenda Spires, leading an entire Girl Scout Troop, pushing her 3-year-old daughter and carrying her 15-month-old son plus two Cabbage Patch Kids, finished a grueling 10-mile Hike/Bike/Run competition.

A kidnapping hoax in Baldwyn, Missouri, brought a king's ransom in national publicity. Cabbage Patch Kid Kimball Madison was said to have been abducted from a local gift shop, whose owner then received three notes demanding $125,000 if she "valued the brat's life." Kimball Madison was recovered — the $125,000 ransom had been raised in Mickey Mouse money — in a barber shop where he was "getting a haircut."

There actually was a Cabbage Patch kidnapping (robbery is a more accurate description) in Virginia Beach, Virginia. Belinda Misty, awaiting adoption at the Thomas House Adoption Center, was abducted (stolen), and it appeared that Debra Naugle, who had been quite taken by the baby, would have to wait three months before she could bring it home, even though the kidnappers were quickly apprehended and the victim rescued. It seems Belinda Misty was needed as a material witness (exhibit) at trial, but the story ended happily, at least for Debra Naugle, when the culprits pleaded guilty prior to their court date and Belinda Misty returned home.

In Westfield, New York, friends and neighbors of Linda Dunn gave a shower for her when she brought home her Cabbage Patch Kid, Cathleen Ellen. Nut cups were fashioned out of Pampers, and gifts included gowns, brush sets, sleepers, bottles, bonnets, bibs, and leotards, plus a book titled "Raising the Only Child."

Parents of Cabbage Patch Kids gave themselves a party at Nell's Harbour Shop in Hilton Head, South Carolina, and brought their "babies" along. Nell Smith, who was dubbed the "head nurse," said the Kids were "among the best behaved I've ever had the pleasure to serve."

Then there was the Great Stuffed Cabbage Roll-Off in

Laguna Beach, California, which was more serious than it sounded. The Stuffed Cabbage Roll-Off was conceived as a folk festival to promote "fun," "family togetherness," and "peace in a troubled world," and was attended by Mrs. John Wayne and Buddy Ebsen, who wrote a song to commemorate the occasion. Honored guests at the festival were a delegation of Cabbage Patch Kids.

People seemed capable of finding an inexhaustible number of social functions at which the Cabbage Patch Kids could play a role. In Bear Lake, California, the Kids and their parents engaged in a tug-of-war with teddy bears and their owners. The bears won. The parents of the Kids seemed to take the loss harder than the Kids themselves. In Sarasota, Florida, children and the Kids were taken to see "Little Miss Marker," a movie starring Walter Matthau, who adopts a little girl during the course of the film. At King Solomon's Mine, an adoption center in Albuquerque, New Mexico, more than a thousand parents (including a father of *three hundred*) took part in a contest, the first prize being a Xavier Roberts' autograph on the behinds of six of their Kids.

Perhaps inspired by the victorious campaign of Effie May for honorary mayor of Palm Harbor, Florida, it was announced that Xavier Roberts' personal Cabbage Patch Kid, Otis Lee, was also running for office. The news was broken in the following manner by the *Cabbage Patch Dispatch*, published by Original Appalachian Artworks:

> Yes, yes, yes, it's true. As unbelievable as it may seem, Otis Lee is on the Campaign trail for the highest office in the land. The office of the President of these United States. Otis Lee, as you all know, is the editor-in-chief of the illustrious CABBAGE PATCH DISPATCH, and a well known figure throughout the nation. When news of this glorious event was made public at BabyLand General, the reaction was overwhelming. Large crowds of cheering Cabbage Patch Kids gathered outside BabyLand General to await the arrival of their World Leader to be. As the Limousine approached (Otis Lee always travels in a Limo), the crowd roared with excitement. People were shouting "Otis Lee is the man for me." As soon as candidate Otis

Lee made his way through the anxious crowd, one of our Political Correspondents, Jane Polly Wolly Doodle, was able to talk to our President to be. THE CABBAGE PATCH DISPATCH is pleased to present, "Otis Lee, The Man With The Plan."

What came next was an interview with Otis Lee, at which he promised to do the following: paint the White House blue; change the nation's capital to Cleveland, Georgia; make Mr. Ed a presidential aide; and appoint dishes, glasses, pots and pans to his cabinet. When asked how he stacked up against Ronald Reagan, Otis Lee said, "Well, I don't have any hair, so I can't dye it, but my cheeks are just as rosy as his, and I love Hollywood."

Otis Lee intended to run with a woman candidate for vice president, Cabbage Patch Kid Sybil Sadie, to run on the Birthday Party, and never to miss the Muppet Show. He confessed to preferring country fairs to foreign affairs, and allowed that red china was okay but blue was better.

The Little Miss Baby Pageant in Tallahassee, Florida, another beauty contest for Cabbage Patch Kids, is almost as hotly contested as its Atlantic City counterpart. The most recent competition was judged by an actual Miss America (1982), and the winner was Karla Melanie. The contests are possible, of course, because each Cabbage Patch Kid is different. They are not produced from a mold, like Barbie or Raggedy Ann or Pac-Man. This technological development was predicted by author Alvin Toffler in "The Third Wave," who thought — correctly, it turned out — that computerization of the assembly line would make the production of one-of-a-kind goods as easy a task as standardized ones. The sex ratio is roughly two girls to one boy, the skin colors of every race are represented, each has different features, and each has a different name. As Toffler forecast, unique, individualized products could be brought within the purchasing range of average citizens.

Dr. Thomas Plaut, assistant chief of behavioral sciences (research branch) for the National Institute of Mental Health, pointed out, however, that "While everybody is wanting something different, everybody is doing the same thing: buying the doll." On the other hand, as *Time* magazine posited, if a merchandizer "could get just *one person* interested in collecting the entire set of Cabbage Kids, he *would never stop buying them.*"

A big difference, besides hand-made quality, between the Coleco Kids and the ones available at Babyland, is the price. Generally, the Coleco versions adopt for between twenty and thirty dollars, while the handmade originals at Babyland and other adoption centers throughout the U.S. start at $125. There is a special "Grand" line, with the girls in mink coats and the boys wearing diamond cufflinks, that go for $1,000 each. One of Xavier Roberts's earliest creations, sans fancy accoutrements, sold to a collector in 1983 for a whopping $3,000.

Before the Madness set in, a Xavier Roberts sales representative showed up at New York's prestigious F.A.O. Schwarz dressed as a nurse to try to persuade buyer Florence Lamuscio to put the department store into the adoption business. The buyer showed the "nurse" to the door. "I knew she couldn't be serious," Ms. Lamuscio said. But then requests began flooding in — 3,000 calls a day — and F.A.O. Schwarz decided the adoption market wasn't beneath its dignity after all.

Counseling is advised for Cabbage Patch Kids whose parents want to change their names and strongly recommended if they are being readopted. Parents are told their babies may become homesick, and that a possible cure is to take them to visit their friends in the Cabbage Patch at Babyland General. And this is the advice offered if one of the Kids should be injured in an accident: "No problem. If Esther should ever need emergency care, Babyland General Hospital has a complete staff of trained Little People doctors and nurses. Simply make her as comfortable as possible (in a suitably sized box with holes punched in it so she can breathe) and send her right off to Babyland. We'll fix her up and send her back to you faster than you can say 'imagicillin.' "

The long and short of it is simply that Xavier Roberts and Coleco were selling fantasy, and the nation was buying it. A "family reunion" was held at Childhood Treasures in Royal Oak, Michigan, with parents conducting a costume party and then taking the Kids to a Chinese dinner. "They're the next best thing to a real child," said one of the guests. "They're cheaper to bring up than real children," said a second. "The

Little People are therapeutic," decided a third. "When you hug one of them, you actually hug yourself."

Maybe so, but Xavier Roberts and Coleco were also hugging each other. They had the perfect product, one that couldn't be manufactured fast enough to meet demand and a huggable $60 million in 1983 sales. Hopes are for a staggering $1 billion in sales in 1984, which would include proceeds from a mind-numbing variety of accessories, including lunch boxes, mugs, towels, books, records, magazines, calendars, a Cabbage Patch folding stroller, a Snuggle-Close Carrier, and an entire wardrobe of clothes — Nightie-Night, School Days, Country Kid, Winter Warmer — plus Cabbage Patch T shirts, shoes, and games. You can purchase tuxedos for the male kids, stunning ballroom gowns for the females. *Fortune* magazine, not given to exaggeration, called it "The billion-dollar Cabbage Patch in Cleveland, Georgia."

The *Wall Street Journal* attributed the popularity of the Cabbage Patch Kids to "people getting tired of electronic games," while Ted Koppel on ABC's "Nightline" said they had the "same appeal as Burger King," which promises to make hamburgers "your way." Xavier Roberts joked "parents were ready for something that didn't cry, wet, or roller skate."

Children treating dolls like real people is hardly anything new. It is the absurd reaction of adults to the Kids that offers the most convincing proof of the dolls' lasting charm. A Dallas, Texas, journalist spotted a rich dowager pushing her Kid, propped up in a shopping cart, through a supermarket aisle. She was arguing out loud with herself about what to buy, and finally deferred to the doll for the decision. And there was the Vermont housewife purchasing an extra seat on an airplane so her "sweet Roosevelt Felix" would have plenty of room.

The country-rock band, Alabama, adopted a Cabbage Patch Kid, Abraham Raymond, and the new baby promptly gave an interview to the *Cabbage Patch Dispatch*. Abraham Raymond revealed that Alabama requires ten buses when it is on tour, that the group writes most of its own music, and that members would never live in Georgia, "their hearts are definitely in Alabama." (This last piece of information proved inaccurate. The singers purchased an expensive condominium in the same Atlanta complex where Xavier Roberts now lives.)

The Oak Ridge Boys adopted four Cabbage Patch Kids. Even Walter Cronkite became a parent. A year before he received the Heisman Trophy, awarded to the top college football player, Herschel Walker adopted a Cabbage Patch Kid named Heisman. "I've needed something to lift my spirits," said the talented, bruising running back, "and I think he is the best possible thing." Heisman, the Cabbage Patch Kid, came in a football jersey emblazoned with the number "¾" on the front.

And the case for the dolls' staying power was further advanced when renowned collectibles expert Gwen Zenerold pronounced the Kids to be one of the "three best modern collectibles" available.

It's doubtful, however, that collectors were responsible for the family reunions, birthday parties, showers, picnic outings, beauty contests, and look-alike competitions organized around the Cabbage Patch Kids. Nor were the collectors the ones talking to their babies, buying airline tickets for them, or building additions on their homes to house them.

Collector or not, "They don't cause you a single gray hair," said SanDee Kinnen of Wyandotte, Michigan, about her Cabbage Patch Kids, "and you know where they are at all times." And, it appears they will be with us for a long time to come.

He Would Say It Hasn't Surprised Him

DOLL BRAWL

Cabbage Patch fever struck again
early this morning when close to
200 people stormed the Longview
Fred Meyer store and battled to
buy one of the chubby-cheeked rag
dolls known as Cabbage Patch Kids.

"They say adopt a Cabbage Patch
Kid. Well, they murdered them in
there today," said Sherry Bullock
of Kelso. She was lucky enough
to snare a doll, but left the store
in tears.

People shoved and pushed and ripped
dolls away from others, she said.

"A man climbed over shelves and over
people to get one. I was terrified.
By the time I got to the checkout
stand I was in tears and couldn't
write the check I was so upset."

Fred Meyer had advertised in The
Daily News Tuesday night that it
would have 72 of "America's most
wanted dolls" on sale today for

$28.96. The dolls have turned
department store aisles into combat
zones, and the scene in Longview
this morning was no exception.

When the doors opened at 9 a.m.,
some 200 people rushed toward the
dolls, snapping them up in a matter
of minutes.

"Store employees backed out of the
way," Bullock said. "They weren't
about to get their heads beat in.

"I hope there's never a food shortage,"
she said. "If they do that over a
doll, what would they do for food?"

Gordon Deeds, Fred Meyer's general
merchandise manager in Portland, said
the pushing and shoving was unfortunate,
but the fight for the dolls caught the
company by surprise. "We thought that
after Christmas there might be less
interest in the dolls."

The Longview store will probably get
more dolls late this week or early
next week, but Fred Meyer isn't going
to advertise them, Deeds said. "We'll
probably put them out just as quietly
as we can."

Longview (Washington) *News* 2/29/84

It wasn't Christmas, 1983 — in fact, it was March 2, 1984 — but
it must have seemed that way to employees of Fred Meyer
department stores throughout the Pacific Northwest. Crowds
of impatient people with eager faces shoved up against display
windows, lines of pushing, jostling customers in front of the
doors, tempers beginning to flare in the frenzied jockeying for
position. The scene was the same at every establishment. "Peo-

ple went bonkers," said Bruce Anderson, assistant manager of the Springfield, Oregon, Fred Meyer store. "One minute and fifty seconds and they were all gone."

One thing a shipment of Cabbage Patch Kids seem guaranteed to supply is excitement. Fred Meyer had advertised a limited supply of the babies at $28.96 each, about three dollars below the regular price, and allotted seventy-two of the Kids to each of its stores in Washington, Oregon, Montana, and Alaska, a total of about five thousand in all. David Lockhart, operations manager for Fred Meyer, thought he had plenty on hand. "Usually after Christmas," Lockhart said, "the demand for the really hot toys subsides. It appears now that the demand has not subsided at all — it appears Coleco will not be able to satisfy the demand this year."

The scene was the same at every store. The seventy-two dolls never lasted more than two minutes, despite the imposition of a two-dolls-per-family limit (most customers purchased a pair). A store manager, asked how many Cabbage Patch Kids would have been enough, couldn't name a figure. "I could have sold thousands today alone," he said, shaking his head. "And then we would have had a battle locking them out."

Xavier wasn't surprised. He had expected it to happen, and preferred to talk about events in Canada, where the same sort of madness had taken place a week earlier than in the Pacific Northwest. Edmonton toy stores had received their first batch of Cabbage Patch Kids since Christmas and, according to the *Edmonton Journal*, they "sold out in minutes."

Sometimes it didn't take that long. At the Macleods store in Bonnie Doon, thirty dolls were offered for sale on a Tuesday morning, including ten black ones. "It didn't matter," said the manager, "they were just ... wh-s-s-sht, they were gone. I didn't even hear a comment as far as that goes. They all went within the first thirty-six seconds of opening the doors. They're just as hot as before Christmas, even more so, I think."

At Tops in Toys in West Edmonton, manager Lena Holowaychuk sold her supply out at close to record speed. "Even before I unpacked them," she said, "they were taking them. It didn't matter, as long as it said Cabbage Patch."

At Eatons Southgate in Edmonton, Canadians proved they could go as wild over the Kids as Americans could. "One fellow," said department manager Casey Jones, "was telling me he had two under his arm. Somebody grabbed one. He didn't even see it go. So he hung onto the one he had for dear life and got out of there."

Perhaps most embarrassed by all of this were newspaper and TV commentators who snickered in their sleeves as they assured all and sundry that the Cabbage Patch craze would be as dead as a Pet Rock once the Christmas season ended; they now find that it is eat-their-words time. The truth is, very few people predicted the Kids would last. Had the commentators done their homework, studied the history of dolls and their nearly universal appeal, they might have glimpsed the real scenario. It would not, in fact, have required any more effort than going back to 1959 and reading about the Barbie doll, or to the turn of the century and the Teddy. Both of these, Coleco and Xavier believe (and especially Xavier has been right all along), will in time be surpassed by the incredible one-of-a-kind Cabbage Patch Kids.

For Xavier, 1983 and 1984 were the years he became a celebrity. He traveled to numerous countries to oversee setting up operations, to give his final product approval to a myriad of retail items, and to be interviewed by newspapers, radio, and television wherever he went. He was a very rich man at a very young age, and it seldom took very long before the conversation wheeled around to his money. Xavier invariably credited it to hard work, and from his mouth the six years it took to acquire the fortune sounded more like six centuries. The time had not passed quickly for the young artist with the vaulting ambition.

But a celebrity he was, and shyly, speaking low, blushing frequently, he patiently answered questions about how he used his money. Expensive cars. The plush condominium in Atlanta. (He had himself whisked to Cleveland in a helicopter when business matters needed attending to.) Traveling. Having a good time. (He was taking friends for a lavish vacation in Jamaica.)

Taxes were a worry, as they always are to the rich. "Keeping the government from taking it all" seemed to require as much time as, in the past, had hustling orders at trade shows and being certain his adoption centers had the sameness of a

McDonald's. It wasn't enjoyable, the constant struggle to keep what he'd made, not fun like building a business against the odds had been; but it would have been madness not to pay close attention to his personal finances. Increasingly he talked about going back to school, *really* studying art, and maybe one day he would.

But the income needed to be monitored and shepherded. *Each day* his fortune increased dramatically, and required more and more of his time. Could that which he had so desired from childhood, now growing to awesome proportions, turn into a monster that would consume him?

The success was phenomenal, and no end was in sight when Xavier was spotted on May 28, 1984, signing autographs at a Washington, D.C., trade show. He looked spiffy in his white sports jacket (though he would never be a clotheshorse, despite his designer labels). He had too much of the mountains in him.

"I hear sales will be a billion dollars this year."

"Yep. A little over."

"What are you gonna do?"

"Travel. Japan. England. The Continent."

"Pleasure?"

"Mostly business. Gotta keep movin'."

Xavier had just come from Hollywood firming up plans for ABC-TV's December 20th prime-time special, "The Cabbage Patch Kids' First Christmas," but there were dozens of other projects in the works. Parker Brothers, producers of "Monopoly," were coming out with *nine* Cabbage Patch-related books: *Xavier's Fantastic Discovery; The Shyest Kid in the Patch; The Big Bicycle Race; The Great Rescue; Making Friends; The Just Right Family;* two dye-cut books; and a coloring book. Parker Brothers were also putting out a Cabbage Patch board game, a Cabbage Patch card game, and a Cabbage Patch electrical game.

But Parker Brothers was doing more. An LP record, "Cabbage Patch Dreams," was released early in 1984, and it hit platinum *before the advertising could begin.* "We expect it to go triple-platinum," Xavier said; and why not? Numerous stores reported they were unable to keep them in stock. The moving forces behind the album were Tom and Steve Chapin, brothers of Harry, the late singer. The album introduced listeners to various of the Cabbage Patch Kids, their friend, a Colonel Casey, and two bad guys, Lavender McDade and Cabbage Jack. Most singers spend their lives fruitlessly hoping for a platinum record, yet all that was needed in this case was the tie-in with the Cabbage Patch phenomenon. A second LP, "Rose Petal Palace," was released in June, with even higher expectations. Incredibly, Parker Brothers had no experience whatever in the record business. "Cabbage Patch Dreams" was the first the company ever put out. Once again it is difficult to miss the irony. A national distributor, like Coleco and Parker Brothers, seeming to rescue Xavier, actually turn out to be the ones reaping the major benefits.

It didn't hurt that the products being turned out in Cleveland, Georgia, continued to be of considerable quality. The first Debonair Bears, sold for $75, were reported to be worth $500 each, and the Bavarian Edition of Cabbage Patch Kids, released early in 1984 at $150 each, shot up almost immediately to $350. Little People Pals went from $75 to between $150 and $200. The fact that Xavier's own babies were increasing in value helped lend an aura of quality to the Coleco product, which on its own merits could hardly be termed shoddy.

Coleco, on the other hand, putting out more than a million dolls a month and totally unable to cope with demand, made the young Georgian's products more desirable. Why not buy the real thing? many customers wondered, since the more than $30 Coleco was charging was a substantial purchase anyway. And with the genuine article, you could avoid the discomfort and hassle.

What the Pacific Northwest witnessed may be the portent of what awaits Christmas, 1984. Coleco is frankly acknowledging that there will be shortages. "If you want a Cabbage Patch Kid," said Coleco spokesperson Barbara Wruck, "and you happen to see one, we highly recommend you get it now." Ms. Wruck firmly denied that, as critics have charged, the shortages are manufactured by Coleco itself to maintain interest and extend the product's life. The latter is not necessary, Xavier concurs, saying the Cabbage Patch Kids are destined to become a part of Americana.

Gimbel's is a department store with decades of experience, and according to company buyer John Young, even when the dolls are in stock, the store knows how to blunt the potential mayhem. "I have never seen such demand for any toy," said Young. "We've only been putting out seventy-two pieces a day — otherwise we'd have riots."

Xavier, at the trade show, was alight with what the future held. "We will begin marketing Koosas in June," he said. "They are made of cloth and are about the same size as the Kids. Like the Kids, each one is different and distinctive." Also, the Koosas were scheduled, since they are pets of indefinable origin, to have their names registered to a kennel with headquarters in New York City. The Koosas, Xavier explained, keeping a straight face, come from the Wykoosa Valley, which is near Cleveland, and "combine the most lovable features of cats and dogs."

The young artist kept a sharp eye on how the big manufacturers marketed his products. He'd had to stop Coleco from putting the Cabbage Patch Kids out in what he thought was an unattractive package, and he kept a similar eye on Parker Brothers and the record venture that hit platinum in its first attempt. The music in "Cabbage Patch Dreams" had a mostly country and western flavor, was aimed at children between ages four and twelve, but the songs also were written with adults in mind. "After all," said Parker Brothers vice president Bruce Jones, "if the first record drives parents nuts, they're not going to buy another one, no matter how much their kids want it."

Xavier and the Cabbage Patch Kids seemed to come along just at the right time where records were concerned. Children's records accounted for seventeen of the forty-seven singles that went gold (500,000 or more copies) in 1983, according to the Recording Industry Association of America. Before, only a very few records for children scaled such lofty heights, and most of these had been put out by Walt Disney Productions.

If the Cabbage Patch craze was started by adults, and it probably was, filtering down to children later, the newest mania — stickers — was launched by youngsters. Of course, Xavier was into stickers. Cabbage Patch Stickers, manufactured by Diamond Toymakers of Niles, Illinois, have ridden in on the crest of the popularity of the dolls, and come in a variety of colors and styles, including scratch-and-sniffs with scents like popcorn, baby powder, and chocolate fudge. There are also holographic stickers that shimmer with dimension, color-me stickers that come with eight grape-scented crayons, and foam-filled vinyl stickers called puffies. Also, a Cabbage Patch Baby Book, a sixteen-page diary that traces the history of a Kid.

What heat was generated by the tremendous commercialization of the Cabbage Patch Kids was mostly absorbed by Coleco. Few if any critics turned their fire on Xavier. He seemed to everyone who talked with him to be unspoiled, modest, a living exception to those who say no more great fortunes can be made in America. The system needed that. It needed people hoping that lightning could strike them, too, that the big monopolies and fortunes had not already cornered everything under the sun. The fact that the odds against hitting a jackpot as large as Xavier's were about the same as winning the Irish Sweeps was irrelevant to those who wanted to believe in the Dream. Besides, Xavier, with the mountains of Georgia written all over him, couldn't have seemed more removed from fast-talking Madison Avenue hucksters trying *too hard* to cash in on a national craze. No, the barbs weren't aimed at Xavier, though he, too, was fully behind the massive commercialization.

Beneath the quiet, slow-talking mountain exterior was an ambition that burned brightly, and translated itself into a quest for money. It was money Xavier sought, not power, though this follows money as surely as night follows day, nor fame, though he was comfortable with this, nor even the accumulation of glittering objects. Money was the standard he used to measure how far he had come from the days of his childhood.

Xavier decided that his ninety-room house didn't fit his needs, though it was difficult to see how it ever could have. Plans were made to turn the house into offices for Original Appalachian Artworks, and to build a factory to manufacture the dolls in the huge backyard. Babyland General Hospital would remain a gift shop — a super-successful one — but the fate of Dr. Neal's old home, which had served as offices, was left up in the air. Alternately, Xavier thought of turning it into a Cabbage Patch Museum or making it into a day-care center for his employees' children.

The Cabbage Patch Kids — the biggest-selling first-year doll in history — may become the biggest selling doll of any year in history in 1984. This is remarkable because, using 1983 as a guide, there is so much competition. In 1983, all but one of the top ten selling non-electronic toys in the United States were dolls or similar creatures, according to Steve Smith, editor of *Toy and Hobby World*. The top five were: Masters of the Universe; GI Joe; Cabbage Patch Kids; Care Bears; and Star Wars action figures. After this came Trivial Pursuit, a board game, Barbie, My Little Pony, Black Star action figures, and Chamkins dolls.

It was virtually impossible to tell which of the top five was actually number one, but there was no doubt which would have been had there been no shortages. "At every store contacted in an informal survey," said the *Los Angeles Times*, "there were callers — dozens, or scores, or hundreds depending on who was asked — who wanted one thing: Cabbage Patch Kids. Said Joe Ferring, owner of Ferring's Thousands of Toys & Games in Bell: 'We could sell them by the carload if we could just get 'em.' "

As David Johnston wrote in that same *Los Angeles Times* article, "In a society where having children is 'in' for the first time in 15 years, a surrogate child made of rags and yarn that comes complete with adoption papers and a promise of a birthday card one year after its purchase has become the most sought-after toy in American history."

Alfred Kahn, senior marketing vice president at Coleco (given much of the credit for Cabbage Patch Madness), himself acknowledges that much of the success was due to Xavier. "When we were first exposed to the Kids, we were struck by the unique concept and its potential opportunity — one-of-a-kind, quality dolls to be merchandised to the mass marketplace. Xavier created something wonderful and we've just made it available to more people. We wanted a long-term commitment to protect our investment, and we got more than that from Cabbage Patch Kids. Coleco committed both dollars and manpower to insure that the execution of this product would be consistent with the quality of Xavier's originals. We knew we had a winner, but we've been overjoyed by the unanimous acceptance by consumers. Extensive consumer research was conducted prior to product launch into the marketplace, and the acceptance of the concept was very positive."

Seven years ago, in 1977, Xavier was struggling to pay his college tuition and adopting out his babies while working at the Unicoi State Park gift shop. Six years ago, 1978, he founded a company, along with five young friends, that few people would have given a chance to succeed. Today he receives income from a bewildering variety of products, only a *few* of which are herein listed: air hardened modeling clay and clay kits; children's melamine dinnerware, including thermoplastic mugs; plastic and vinyl lamps; night lights and switch plates; shoe bags; umbrellas; scarves; sun glasses; checkbook covers; plastic trophies; name plates; clothes hangers; magnets; key chains; pin-on buttons; combs; brushes; mirrors; pencils; pillows; rulers; erasers; note pads; pens; study kits; paint-by-number sets; pencil-by-number sets; crayon-by-number sets; poster art sets; sweaters; Halloween costumes; girls and boys sleepwear; socks; colorforms; Shrinky Dinks; sewing cards; rubdown transfers; puzzleforms; children's toiletries and cosmetics; swimwear; greeting cards; gift wrap; wooden and paper school supply boxes; photo albums; stationery; placemats; baby books; gum-backed paper stickers; calendars; sticker books; logo stickers; rain coats; rain jackets; rain ponchos; wall covering; bibs; trainer cups; stamp sets; tea sets; baby care sets; chalk boards; bulletin boards; tooth brushes; bubble pipes; pails; shovels; children's jewelry and hair accessories; tote bags; shoulder bags; wallets; backpacks; luggage; portable table lamps; hanging lamps; thermal underwear; panties; snack trays; shelving; puzzles; shoe skates; skate bags; watches; clocks; microphones; headsets; radios; cassette recorder players; phonographs; intercoms; walkietalkies; belts; suspenders; hats; gloves; mittens; cotton caps; slippers; party supplies; blanket sleepers; bicycles; picture frames; cookie jars; music boxes; bedding; towels; throw rugs; draperies; curtains; ceramic vases; binders; figurines; and bells.

Even for individual items, the clothes for Cabbage Patch Kids often were more expensive than clothes for a real kid.

Nor was it always wise to buy regular children's outfits for the Kids, because they are proportioned differently from children. "A lot of kids," said Kathleen McNamara, a merchandise associate at the Chevy Chase, Maryland, Woodward & Lothrop department store, "come in to buy clothes for their dolls, but they don't fit. They just hang off them."

The enterprising Xavier did offer a solution. He had published a book of patterns, cost $5, including those for a dress, panties, pants, a knit top, shirt, cap, and shoes. The book offered twenty-six outfits, with many more available through mixing and matching.

The billion dollars in sales of Cabbage Patch Kids and related products projected for 1984 needs to be put in sharper perspective. Coleco, the giant whom Xavier sought out to get wider distribution for his babies, had $178 million in sales in 1981, almost *six times less* than what Xavier himself expects just three years later. In this sense, Xavier, the "little guy," has already shown his heels to one of the largest toy manufacturers in the world.

Xavier's personal success, coming so rapidly, is almost as phenomenal as the 1983 Christmas Cabbage Patch Phenomenon itself. And in many ways he is in a better position than Coleco. To grow even richer, he doesn't even have to gamble with most products. Except for what is manufactured by Original Appalachian Artworks, no expenditure whatever is required on his part for many of the products that bear the Cabbage Patch name. If a company wants to use that name (and obviously many do) it has to pay *Xavier*, and continue to pay each time the item sells. If a company putting out a lunch pail with the Cabbage Patch logo happens to fail, an unlikely prospect, at least at this time, the licensee is the one down the drain, not Xavier.

Can the endorsement of products by Cabbage Patch Kids be very far away? What would it be worth to Wheaties, for example, if baseball "star" Tyler Bo recommended that children eat them? Why not a candy bar named after Tyler Bo? Or Otis Lee saying all the Kids in the Patch liked to get together at Wendy's?

Xavier was hardly reticent about what he considered the true state of affairs to be. In June, 1983, he appeared at a packed press conference in Boston with a number of Coleco executives. "I'm pleased to welcome Coleco," he said, "and the other Cabbage Patch Kids' licensees into the Babyland family, and I know they'll put the same attention and commitment to quality into their products as I put into my original soft sculpture babies."

Thus, in Xavier's own words, Coleco was joining Babyland! It was, as a cartoonist depicted in another matter, a case of the goldfish thinking he could swallow the whale!

Yet, again, how far wrong was he? Coleco, though it didn't know to what extent, was in trouble. The Cabbage Patch Kids would soon be on their way into the stratosphere.

One surefire way exists for Xavier to increase his already formidable fortune, and that is to take his company public. It would inject a massive infusion of cash, and maintaining a controlling interest would pose no problem. This tack has propelled other men into billionaire status (H. Ross Perot, the computer tycoon, for one), into an ultra-elite club to which the young artist fully intends to belong.

Whatever the denouement, years down the line, the fortune seems destined to grow and grow, as the Disney dynasty did, whether or not the creator is around to tend it. The important thing is Xavier was around at the beginning — he *was* the beginning — and he's had quite a run from a dead-broke, poorly educated mountain boy with a cheering section of one, his mother Eula, to being the generator, at age twenty-eight, of a *billion* dollars in sales.

He would tell you it hasn't surprised him at all.

I want to thank Jim Black, Wayne Stokes, Kevin Howe, Bob Frese, Jim Gosdin, David Hurst, Tillie Harrison, Bill Dear, Joanne Schein, Carla Lehrmann, Danny Owens, Kathleen Ferguson, Julie Koch, Freddie Goff, Marsha Davis, Candace Albertson, Steve Freeman, Ann Hinson, Gerald Bane, Brenda Bane, Laura Meier, Judyth Rigler, John Reeves, Anita Reeves, Leonard McBrayer, Bess McBrayer, Kim Blackledge, Terri Hoffman, William Hoffman III, Joe Hoffman, John Hoffman, Sister Mary Anne Lucy, Ethan Lewis, Micah Lewis, and especially Lea Lewis, who loaned us Diana Tallulah.